DIVINE MONEY SPELLS
Jump Start Your Spiritual Economic Stimulus Package

By
Dragonstar
&
Rev. William A. Oribello

INNER LIGHT PUBLICATIONS

DIVINE MONEY SPELLS
Dragonstar ~ William Oribello

Divine Money Spells
Jump Start Your Spiritual Economic Stimulus Package

Dragonstar & William Alexander Oribello

ISBN-10: 1606110640
ISBN-13: 978-1606110645
Nonfiction – Metaphysics

Timothy Green Beckley: Editorial Director
Carol Rodriguez: Publishers Assistant
Tim Swartz: Associate Editor
Sean Casteel: Editorial Assistant
William Kern: Editorial Assistant
Cover Art: Tim Swartz

1.   Oribello, William, Dragonstar, Paranormal, Magical Arts, Metaphysics – Nonfiction

I. Title: Divine Money Spells: Jump Start Your Spiritual Economic Stimulus Package

133'.4

For free catalog write:
Global Communications
P.O. Box 753
New Brunswick, NJ 08903

Free Subscription to Conspiracy Journal E-Mail Newsletter
www.conspiracyjournal.com

DIVINE MONEY SPELLS
Dragonstar ~ William Oribello

DIVINE MONEY SPELLS
Dragonstar ~ William Oribello

DIVINE MONEY SPELLS
Dragonstar ~ William Oribello

CHAPTER ONE - WHAT IS MAGICK?

Just what exactly is Magick? Unfortunately, there is no single, correct answer to this question. You will find answers as varied as the belief systems which incorporate magical elements and the people who practice within each system.

In seeking a definition of the term, perhaps we should look no further than the most mundane of sources:

"It is the art of producing a desired effect or result through the use of various techniques as incantations that presumably assure human control of supernatural agencies or the forces of nature." - **Webster English Dictionary**

Or we can defer to old philosophers and alleged magicians for meaning. Aleister Crowly defined Magick as:

"The Science and Art of causing Change to occur in conformity with Will."

In **The Lemegeton (Lesser Book of Solomon, the King)**, we find:

"Magick is the highest, most Absolute, most Divine Knowledge of natural Philosophy, advanced in its works and wonderful operations by a right understanding of the inward and occult (hidden) virtue of things; so that true agents being applied to proper patients, strange and admirable effects will hereby be produced. Whence magicians are profound and diligent searchers into Nature; they, because of their skill, know how to anticipate an effect, the which to the vulgar shall seem to be a miracle."

Or one of these might well do:

DIVINE MONEY SPELLS
Dragonstar ~ William Oribello

"Magick is the traditional science of the secrets of nature which has been transmitted to us by our ancestors of the priesthood of the Magi." — Eliphas Levi

"Magick is the application of human Will (originating in the Soul) to the fast evolution of the Living forces of nature." -Gerard Encausse

"The art of White magic is the art of using so-called Spiritual or invisible forces, to obtain visible results." -Franz Hartmann

A more contemporary definition of describes Magick as a kind of energy which pervades the cosmos. Others see it as a psychic tool by which we may influence the material world using symbols and ritual. Many see it as a means of coming to unite with the divine; some consider it to be the exercise of will or Will, or the manipulation of reality.

In other words, only the individual can determine what Magick is or isn't for themselves. Magic is exactly what you believe it to be, for it requires your belief to be anything at all. As one wise and unknown sage put it: "Magick is Within You!"

There is a power in the universe. This power is the inexplicable force behind the wonders that early humans encountered. The Earth, the solar systems, the stars - all that is manifest - is a product of this power.

This power is also within all things. It is within humans, plants, stones, colors, shapes and sounds. This power can be roused and concentrated.

Power is "awakened" and moved through ritual dance or other physical movement; through sounds such as music or chanting; through manipulation of various objects through concentration or magical visualization.

DIVINE MONEY SPELLS
Dragonstar ~ William Oribello

This power can be "programmed" with specific vibrations or energies to affect a specific result. This result is the spell's purpose. It may be to speed healing, attract money or to bring love into one's life. The power is programmed through the magician's visualization or the tools and ritual pattern chosen.

This power can be moved and directed.

That power which exists within humans can be moved to other humans and to places and objects, and also transferred from objects to human beings. It is moved and directed through visualization and with the use of tools such as images, wands, swords, pointed fingers and concentration.

This power, once moved, has an affect on its target. Once this power arrives at its destination, it changes the object, person or place. It accomplishes this due to its specific energies. The method by which the power changes its target is determined during ritual or is left up to circumstances at the time of its arrival.

This, in short, is the rationale of Magick. Many of its practitioners aren't consciously aware of these ideas. Others certainly have different explanations and ideas concerning Magick. However, broadly speaking, the only effective spells and rituals are those that are so constructed that any sufficiently involved magician, properly performing it, will raise energy, give it purpose, direct it toward its goal and affect its target.

THE DIFFERENCE BETWEEN MAGICK AND PRAYER

It is often a mistaken belief that inanimate "things" possess magickal powers. But, with the exception of crystals, spiritual or magickal objects are just that, objects. They have no power of their own; they are a means of focusing one's energy on the task at hand.

DIVINE MONEY SPELLS
Dragonstar ~ William Oribello

This statement doesn't mean that certain herbs, roots, minerals and scents are extraordinarily helpful in harnessing the powers of the mind and universe. Creating "magick" takes vision, time and dedication. Yes, people do dab a few drops of gambling oil on themselves and walk into casinos and win big. But the truth be known, this is the exception more than the rule. Getting consistent results in your magickal undertakings requires effort, which is why they call it spiritual "work."

Two means through which one may attempt to change their circumstances are Magick and Prayer. Both refuse to accept weakness as a limit of endeavor or to accept the status quo as normal. Both require belief or faith in "the process" in order to be successful. But, this is where the comparisons end. In order to determine which way of tackling a situation is best suited to the individual, it is helpful to discern what each is in its own terms.

Prayer is not a power, but a request. It is not so much a technique as a conversation. To pray is to say "No" to despair and "Amen" to the "Yes" of the Divine. So, it is the means to end problems and open the door to joy.

We cannot guarantee what Spirit will do with our prayers. This is good because it means prayer cannot make bad things happen.

"The prayer of a righteous man is powerful and effective."

(James 5:16).

By the same token, we do not know how our requests will be addressed, if at all. Prayer is also deeper than words.

"Likewise the Spirit also helpeth our infirmities: for we know not what we should pray for as we ought: but the Spirit itself maketh intercession for us with groanings which cannot be uttered." (Romans 8:26-27).

8

DIVINE MONEY SPELLS
Dragonstar ~ William Oribello

If we use Prayer as the basis of our Spiritual undertakings we must understand that it is not our will which becomes manifest - but that of the Divine. We may not get exactly what we ask for. We may get more or less. The belief that the Spirit works in our best interest implies it does not matter. If you do not ask, you do not receive. If you do not receive, it was not meant to be.

In contrast to Prayer is Magick...the belief that supernatural forces can be controlled, influenced and manipulated by executing a ritualistic formula, either physical or verbal.

The two key components of this definition are A. Ritual and B. Manipulation. In order for Magick to be effective, it must manipulate energy. This may be the Creator energy, an herbal energy, a spiritual force, planetary energy, etc.

It must also adhere to the Webster's Dictionary definition of ritual: "A prescribed procedure for conducting religious ceremonies."

When one makes the attempt to manipulate or coerce any energy into performing his/her own will, Magick has been performed. This is what takes Magick above and beyond Prayer. The magician, not the Divine decides upon the desired outcome.

Magickal rituals do incorporate prayer-like incantations or spoken requests. However, in this context the magician understands he can constrain, coerce, and force the divinity to do his will. Many religions use sacrifices and elaborate doxologies to induce God to favor requests, grant wishes and perform miracles upon demand. Is this Magick? Yes. Religion and Magick are not mutually exclusive. While often unspoken, they frequently walk hand in hand.

When considering ritual and magic as a means of influencing the outcome of any situation, this is probably the most important question one can ask herself. At the least, magickal rituals require three basic components:

1. Statement of Intention ~ What do you want? What is the goal you plan to achieve? Is it attainable? What will you do on the physical or mundane plane to back up the work? What is your time frame? How will you convey these goals to your Spirit or source of power?

2. Raising Energy ~ How will you connect with your Spiritual Alignments or tap into Universal Energy? Invocation? Evocation? Chanting? Drumming? Dancing? Harnessing an Element? Incantation? Meditation? Prayer?

3. Projecting Energy Towards Goal ~ Once you have raised the energy or called the Spirit how will you convey your will and target? How do you get the energy to where it needs to go?

If you do not know what you want and/or do not understand the method or means of raising and projecting Energy than you probably are not ready for much spell work. These three simple steps are the heart of every ritual. The technique that is highly suggested for most problems that require ritual should also includes Prayer. Pray to the Divine for assistance with your Magick spells and for a successful outcome without any harm to others.

DAYS OF THE WEEK – MAGICKAL CORRESPONDENCES

Astrologers, magicians, occultists and spiritualists have long considered planetary influences to be an important consideration when determining the time to cast a spell. Each day of the week is ruled by a planet that possesses specific magickal influences.

SUNDAY: Health; Prosperity; Leadership; Joy, Male Fertility; Protection - Do spellcrafting that involves

DIVINE MONEY SPELLS
Dragonstar ~ William Oribello

Fathers & Husbands, Peace, Harmony, Influence people in High Places - Court Work.

MONDAY: Emotions; Women's Mysteries; Dreams; Reconciliation; Receptivity; Voyages; Female Fertility - Do spells involving the subconscious, healing emotional wounds, children, small animals, mothers, sisters, female partners, wives, instincts.

TUESDAY: Conquest; Commanding: Controlling; Power over Enemies - Craft spells that involve Courage, Immediate Action, Victory or Break Negative Spells.

WEDNESDAY: Aid Spiritual and Psychic Awareness; Divination; Communication - Do spells for Mental Issues, Learning, Addictions, Perception, Artistry, Creativity.

THURSDAY: Growth; Expansion; Generosity - Do spells for Prosperity, Money, Business, Ambition, Male Fertility.

FRIDAY: Love; Pleasure; Friendship; Beauty - Do spells for attracting sex, increasing romance.

SATURDAY: Rid Obstacles; Overcomes Blockages; Clear One's Path - Do spells to remove bindings, Purification.

MOON PHASES

For centuries it has been recognized that the Moon's phase is important to what type of Magick will be performed. From New Moon to Dark Moon, each period in the moon's development brings with it a special energy for that lunar cycle.

From scientific study, we know the Moon affects the ocean tides, animals, plant development and even human behavior. It is also accepted within the magical community that the Moon can and does create fluctuations on the psychic

DIVINE MONEY SPELLS
Dragonstar ~ William Oribello

energies within each of us. So, it only makes sense that the Moon would have a direct influence on our magickal and spiritual workings.

Simply put, there are two cycles and three phases during each cycle. Below are descriptions of these phases and standard recommendations for the type of magic to be performed within each. The moon is known by many names, myths and legends. Respective schools, sects and orders have varying interpretations of Moon Magick according to their own beliefs.

SIMPLE MOON MAGICK

There are two general phases of the moon. In working moon Magick on its most basic level, one can look solely at the WAXING and WANING of the moon.

A simple rule of thumb you may choose to follow states that Drawing is conducted during the WAXING MOON and Removing is conducted during the WANING MOON. If you never get more involved in lunar cycles, you still take advantage of the moon's power by adhering to these simple principles.

WAXING MOON

To Draw Something to you like money or love you make prayers or set spells during the WAXING MOON.

* Appearance - The moon is growing into a FULL MOON. A waxing moon shows a LIGHT colored crescent on the RIGHT side of the Moon.

* Magickal Qualities - Used for attraction magic, love spells, protection and healing. The perfect time for abundance, wishes, new projects, growth, expansion and increasing knowledge, spirituality and fertility.

DIVINE MONEY SPELLS
Dragonstar ~ William Oribello

WANING MOON

To Send Away Trouble or Remove Evil you make prayers or set work during the WANING MOON.

* Appearance - The moon is getting smaller after being a FULL MOON. A waning moon shows a DARK colored crescent on the RIGHT side of the Moon. In other words, the left of the moon is LIGHT and the RIGHT is DARK.

* Magickal Qualities - Used for banishing and rejecting those things that influence us in a negative way. Negative emotions, diseases, ailments, and bad habits can all be dealt with during this moon phase. Purification and House Cleansings should be performed at this time.

MORE ADVANCED MOON MAGICK

A complete lunar phase takes about 29 1/2 days to complete. Beginning at the NEW MOON, we see the total absence of the Moon in the night sky. The WAXING or the increasing of the moon follows as it grows into a FULL MOON. From this point, the moon decreases in size during the WANING phase of the moon. The cycle is complete with the DARK MOON or when no moon is visible.

Remember that the Moon rises about 48 minutes later than the day before as it works itself through the lunar cycle. Moon rises can and do occur in the day - so never think Moon Magick is always conducted at night. If you are serious about doing work or conducting ritual in conjunction with the Moon, put this old rule to memory.

The NEW MOON always rises at sunrise
And the FIRST QUARTER at noon.
The FULL MOON always rises at sunset
And the LAST QUARTER at midnight.

DIVINE MONEY SPELLS
Dragonstar ~ William Oribello

The NEW MOON, FULL MOON and DARK MOON are all important stops in the Moon's monthly cycle. Many people use these days for special workings, believing they are more powerful. It is up to you to decide which phase works best for you for the types of spells you wish to cast.

NEW MOON

* Appearance - The new moon appears to be totally dark or that there is no moon out at night.

* Magickal Qualities - The NEW MOON introduces the WAXING MOON phase of the lunar cycle. Some say not to begin work until the actual WAXING CRESCENT is visible. Used for personal growth, healing and blessing of new projects or ventures. It's also a good time to cleanse and consecrate ritual tools.

FULL MOON

* Appearance - The moon appears totally light.

* Magickal Qualities - The FULL MOON is the culmination of the WAXING MOON (increasing) phase. After the FULL MOON the WANING MOON (decreasing) phase begins. Some say you may perform FULL MOON magic three days prior to and after the actual full moon. Others believe rituals must be started or in process during the actual hour of the full moon. Any spells may be cast during the Full Moon - especially protection and divination.

DARK MOON

* Appearance - The dark moon appears totally dark or that there is no moon out at night. It occurs 3 days prior to the New Moon.

DIVINE MONEY SPELLS
Dragonstar ~ William Oribello

* Magickal Qualities - Typically no work is performed during this time. Some feel the Dark Moon phase continues until the actual WAXING MOON crescent is visible in the sky. Others believe this period officially ends at the hour of the NEW MOON.

IS IT WRONG TO WANT PROSPERITY?

We've all heard it – we're living in some tough economic times. We can get creative and call it a financial hurricane, or an economic tornado, but no matter what, most of us are affected by it.

Why did this happen? How can we stop it? The first thing that we need to understand is that money is really nothing more than pure energy. We do attract whatever we have in our lives at any given time, so if we want more money, we have to place all of our attention and focus on having more money, not focus on what we don't have.

Wealth and prosperity comes from a state of mind, a projection of energy; we have to open up our minds and accept what the universe and the gods and goddesses have to give us. We must be willing and accepting of the energy that we have to attract whatever it is that we really want.

Those who have prosperity are not thinking about what they don't have; they're thinking of what they do have, and what they also want to obtain. They have turned on their energy to allow wealth and prosperity to flow freely to them. They have stopped worrying about not having financial freedom, and they have positive energy which attracts wealth.

With this thought in mind, we're going to set about creating some positive energy which will attract money into our lives. These Divine money spells will manifest more money into your life from every corner of Creation.

DIVINE MONEY SPELLS
Dragonstar ~ William Oribello

Magick is there for those who desire to practice it. Magick serves the need for individual humans to take control of their lives. This isn't through the manipulation of nature, through domination or commandeering. Instead, magicians work with nature's powers and their own personal energy.

Magick is a power of the people, not of organized religion, nor politics, authority or groups. This has sustained it through the millennia. Among some of its practitioners it is a continuance of tradition and culture, a link with ancestors long gone, an affirmation of cultural worth. This, too, is a reason for its survival.

Remember that Magick is the manipulation of energy, a thought is a form of energy and a visualization is an even stronger form of energy. Your visualization can be a method used to intensify further and direct your will. Your visualization can be the method by which you control the magickal energy you have produced. You must know what you want. You must see it. You must feel the high energy flow. You must direct it.

This book of *Divine Money Spells* was written with the help of personal papers and other notes left by the late metaphysical teacher William Alexander Oribello. As well, some parts of this book were also compiled by the spiritual medium Aurora Thyme as she communicated with the spirit of Rev. Oribello for his book *The Mediumship of Spirit.*

With practice and the proper state of mind, the spells contained within this book can help you achieve the happiness and peace of mind that the Creator wants all of his children to have. There is nothing wrong with wanting to be happy...we were not put on this planet to suffer. If you want to be happy, then take the first steps to claim your right to be happy and make it happen.

DIVINE MONEY SPELLS
Dragonstar ~ William Oribello

DIVINE MONEY SPELLS
Dragonstar ~ William Oribello

CHAPTER TWO – GETTING STARTED

Many of the spells contained within this book would be categorized as Folk Magick...Magick that has been practiced by people just like you and me since the beginning of time. Folk Magick is not associated with any religion, yet many spells associated with it are often used in conjunction with Biblical passages and the Psalms.

Folk Magick was born in an age of mystery. Thousands of years ago, nature was a strange force, points of light hung overhead in the sky. Invisible forces ruffled hair and kicked up dust storms. Water fell from the sky. Powerful forces, inconceivable to humans, sent flashes of light from the skies, blasting trees into ashes. Women miraculously bore young. All that lived eventually died. Blood was sacred, food was sacred. Water, the Earth, plants, animals, the wind and all that existed was infused with power.

Folk Magick slowly developed from these beginnings. Every group, every tribe had its own forms of ritual. Folk Magick differed from structured religion and organized Magick; this was the realm of personal Magick, performed for personal reasons. A woman dressed a wound with a plantain leaf that she had gathered with her left hand to increase its healing properties. The fisherman rubbed his bone hooks with flowers to attract fish. Love-sick teens gathered heart-shaped stones and presented them to ones that they desired.

These simple rituals continued to be used for many thousands of years, particularly in isolated, rural areas. With the growing tide of organized religions, many of the old ways of Folk Magick were forgotten. Others were altered to outwardly conform to the new religions. The Magick that could not be made to conform to the new religion was practiced in secret.

However, Folk Magick never died out completely, it continued to exist, handed down from generation to generation.

DIVINE MONEY SPELLS
Dragonstar ~ William Oribello

Throughout the Far, Near and Middle East, in Africa, Polynesia and Australia, in Central and South America, in rural sections of North America such as the Ozarks, in Hawaii and even in parts of Europe, Folk Magick still existed and was practiced, albeit in secret.

During the 1960's, Folk Magick saw a rebirth. The youth movement in the United States rebelled against rigid social codes and Christian ideals. Some young persons turned to Buddhism, Zen and other Eastern teachings. Others became entranced with what little they could learn of spells, charms, herb Magick, tarot cards, amulets and talismans. Countless popular books and articles appeared, revealing this once public knowledge to a new generation dissatisfied with their purely technological lives. Folk Magick constitutes the bulk of ancient and modern magickal techniques practiced by individuals to improve their lives.

What Folk Magick is not is almost as important as what it is. It isn't the "Devil's work." It isn't "Satanism." It doesn't involve sacrifices of humans or animals. It isn't talking to spirits or calling up "demons." It isn't dark, dangerous or evil. Folk Magick isn't anti-Christian or anti-religion. It is a tool with which people can transform and improve their lives. When normal means fail, when all efforts have brought no results, people will often turn to Folk Magick. This is the way it has been for centuries.

At the heart of Folk Magick is the spell. This is simply a ritual in which various tools are purposefully used, the goal is fully stated, and energy is moved to bring about the needed result. Spells are usually misunderstood by non-practitioners. In popular thought, all you need to perform magic is a spell, or maybe a magic wand. In Folk Magick, spells, words, chants, gestures with tools, are the outer form only. The real Magick, the movement of energy, is within the magician. No demonic power flows to help the spell-caster. Instead, the magician – by correctly performing a genuine spell, builds up the power within. At the proper time this power is released to work in manifesting the spell.

DIVINE MONEY SPELLS
Dragonstar ~ William Oribello

Effective spells are designed to facilitate this energy. So, while "true" spells do exist, the actual Magick isn't in the words or tools, it is within the folk magician.

Although personal power, that which resides within the magician, is the most potent force at work in Folk Magick, practitioners borrow freely from the spells and rituals of various cultures, using a wide variety of magickal equipment. These tools are used to help focus the mental energies and put the magician in the proper frame of mind to perform the spell. Folk Magick also affects the collective unconscious, removing the filters we put upon ourselves every day. However, no matter how many times the Magick is performed, it will not work unless you support the Magick with action. Magick works by using coincidence, so be alert when the conjunctions start to happen.

Folk Magick spells can be as simple as reciting a short chant over a silver coin while placing it between two green candles in order to draw money; forming and retaining an image of the needed result in the mind; or placing a quartz crystal in a sunny window for protection purposes. To perform effective Magick, three necessities must be present: *The Need, the Emotion and the Knowledge.*

HOW TO CHOOSE PROPER WORDS OF POWER

When you practice Magick, you must clearly state your need. State all dimensions of your need (money without harm to others; complete protection, rather than just physical protection; etc.). If possible, mention some of the tools that you've decided to use in the spell in your words of power or magickal rhyme.

Indeed, for some spells, these words may help you to structure the entire rhyme or chant. Use hypnotic words, those beginning with S or containing a Z for psychic-

DIVINE MONEY SPELLS
Dragonstar ~ William Oribello

awareness, and good luck spells. Use potent, strong words for money and wealth spells.

Match the words to the type of ritual you're composing. Don't expect the words to simply flow from you. Work at it and work with them. Your psychic mind knows what you need.

A good example of a simple, yet very effective Magick spell is intended to bring about a personal desire, such as a new love or much needed money.

You need to visualize what it is that you desire...some quick cash, a new job, good luck in business. Next, close your eyes and repeat these words three times.

Earth and Sea,
Keep harm from me.
Wind and Fire,
Bring my desire.

Repeat this chant once a day for three days. Feel free to try your own personal variations...remember, the Magick comes from within <u>YOU</u>, not from the chant. It is <u>YOUR</u> desire that manipulates the mystic energies of Creation.

Another spell that uses power words for obtaining fast money is the following: On a Friday during the Waxing Moon anoint a green candle with appropriate money-drawing oil, such as Patchouli, Jasmine, or Cinnamon.

Take the candle and place in a holder. Place a brand new shiny penny in front of the holder and repeat the following chant three times:

Money, Money come to me, $100 is what I need.
With harm to none and help to many, multiply
now this shiny penny!

Now light your candle and gaze into its flame, strongly visualizing the needed money coming to you. Continue with this visualization for as long as possible. After the candle has burned down completely, bury any remaining wax on your property and carry the penny with you to reinforce your magickal intention.

WORDS OF POWER FOR MONEY AND/OR MATERIAL ABUNDANCE

Light a candle, burn some cinnamon incense (money drawing) and say these words on seven days during the Waxing Moon and on the night of the Full Moon. Keep it up until you have what is needed.

There is One Power, Which is perfect abundance and fulfillment. And I (your name), am a perfect manifestation of this Power.

The Power, working for me and through me, provides for me all the abundance and fulfillment which is rightfully mine.

I draw to me and create in my life all that I need in the World of Form to fulfill my needs.

This may come specifically in the form of money, I hereby realize all cause, effect, manifestation, form and essence and any channel within me, Which may have been preventing the appropriate flow of abundance in my life.

I draw upon the balance of resources in the Universe, For the good of all, According to the free will of all,

DIVINE MONEY SPELLS
Dragonstar ~ William Oribello

And I affirm my own wisdom in understanding my needs, and how to fulfill them.

I call to me just enough resources, Knowing I deprive none, and am not deprived myself, I have just enough. And so must it be.

MONEY, MONEY SPELL

This may be done at any time, but preferably at the same time each day or night. You will need a Green Candle and a White Candle. The Green candle represents the money, and the white candle represents you.

Make sure you annoint the candles with oil first, thinking of your desire for money to come to you. Set the candles on your alter or table 9 inches apart. After doing this say...

Money, money come to me
In abundance three times three
May I be enriched in the best of ways
Harming none on its way
This I accept, so mote it be
Bring me money three times three!"
Repeat this for nine days. Each day move the white candle one inch closer to the green candle. When the candles touch, your spell is finished. Make sure you visualize the money pouring in from the universe.

DIVINE MONEY SPELLS
Dragonstar ~ William Oribello

COLTSFOOT WEALTH SPELL

For wealth and prosperity for a year, take the husk from an ear of corn and put a dollar bill along with a note written on parchment...

Oh, dear god of luck, money is like muck,
not good except it be spread.

Spread some here at-------------(write in your address).
Thanks be to thee. Amen.

Sign your name. Sprinkle the dollar bill and note with coltsfoot leaves. Roll the husk up and tie together with green string or ribbon. Hang the token up above the entryway with green cord. That husk should bring riches into your home or business by the bushel.

TOSSING A COIN IN WATER FOR LUCK

It is a tradition in many parts of the world to toss a coin in a well, brook or sea for luck. Here are three traditional rhymes to use to get what you wish for.

I THROW A COIN INTO A WELL
SOON MY LUCK WILL GROW AND SWELL

I THROW A COIN INTO THE SEA
MANY MORE WILL COME TO ME

I THROW A COIN INTO A CREEK
I'LL GET ALL MONEY THAT I SEEK.

DIVINE MONEY SPELLS

Dragonstar ~ William Oribello

PENNY FINDING MAGIC

Everyone knows the rhyme: "See a penny, pick it up, all the day you'll have good luck." It is actually rooted in real folk magic. Finding a penny (once a real bit of money) means that money will come to you as well as good luck. My marking the occasion with a real acknowledgement, that potential good luck can be made a reality. Here are some variations, some traditional, some not:

SEE A PENNY PICK IT UP, ALL THIS DAY I'LL HAVE GOOD LUCK!

*IF THE HEAD IS FACING YOU,
WHAT YOU WISH WILL SOON COME TRUE!*

*IF IT IS THE BACK YOU SEE,
WITH YOUR MONEY GO BE FREE!*

*IF A SILVER COIN IS FOUND
ALL YOU INVEST WILL BE SOUND.*

*IF A COIN IS AT YOUR FEET
SOON YOU WILL SOME MONEY GREET.*

According to ancient traditions, money found in different places has correspondence to the four elements:

MONEY FOUND IN EARTH NEW PROFIT WILL GIVE BIRTH

MONEY FOUND IN WATER GIFTS TO SON OR DAUGHTER

*MONEY FOUND IN AIR SPEND IT WITHOUT CARE!
MONEY FOUND NEAR FIRE WILL GRANT YOUR TRUE DESIRE!*

DIVINE MONEY SPELLS
Dragonstar ~ William Oribello

SPRING TREE MONEY SPELL

Get a small tree to plant; a Birch tree or an Oak is best. Take a silver coin you have been carrying for at least a week and, on a full moon in the spring, plant the tree and put the coin among the roots of the tree, saying:

HERE TAKES ROOT THE MONEY TREE
EACH SEED IS GOLD EACH LEAF A BILL
MAKING EASY ALL I SEE
EVERY GREEN-NEED IT WILL FILL
SO IT IS
AND SO WILL BE
BY MOTHER EARTH
AND BY THIS TREE
JUSTICE AND CASH WILL BE
FOREVER HERE, FOREVER FREE!

Water this tree every day until it flourishes. Repeat the spell every time you water it. This will guarantee you prosperity as long as you take good care of the tree.

MOON SPELL TO GAIN MONEY

Fill a cup half-full of water and drop a silver coin into it. Position the cup so that the light of the Full Moon shines into the water. Gently sweep your hands just above the surface, symbolically gathering the Moon's silver while saying:

Lovely Lady of the Moon, bring to me your wealth right soon. Fill my hands with silver and gold. All you give, my hands can hold.

Repeat three times then pour the water upon the earth.

DIVINE MONEY SPELLS
Dragonstar ~ William Oribello

EASY MONEY SPELL

Take a dollar bill and dab some cedar-wood oil on it and wrap it around three magnets and you'll have yourself a little money magnet. Recite the following:

Money, money, come to me.
It is my will so mote it be!

Prosperity is a belief and your mind is the magnet, all that is necessary for you to change your current economic situation is to change your mind and to develop a different point of view about yourself and your life! You can have all that you need and then some if you just give yourself the permission to be free from the poverty consciousness that you have spent a lifetime building and reinforcing!

Money is pure energy, and prosperity is a state of mind, in order for you to be prosperous in this lifetime you first have to release yourself from the mental bonds of poverty...and yes poverty is a state of mind. If you can let go of the idea that prosperity and wealth are out of your reach and open your mind up to what the universe holds in store for you, prosperity will be yours for the taking.

WEALTH AND PROSPERITY ON A SUNDAY

For this spell you will need: One piece of money attracting crystal, Citrine works very well for this spell. You will also need one gold candle - one silver coin - one oil burner and Frankincense essential oil.

On the first stroke of Midnight light the oil burner and the gold candle. Hold the silver coin in your right hand (this is your receiving hand).

DIVINE MONEY SPELLS
Dragonstar ~ William Oribello

As you gaze into the flame of the candle repeat the Angel Invocation:

Archangel Michael I invoke thee to grant my wish tonight.
Grant me my wish and ease my plight.
Money luck not greed enough to fulfil my needs.
Grant my wish and I will remember.
To give as I have received.
So Mote It Be.

Thank the Archangel for helping you and allow the candle to burn down.

Keep the silver coin in your purse or wallet along with the Citrine, this will ensure you will always have enough money to fulfill your needs.

SPELL TO GET WHAT YOU WANT

Take a horseshoe and put it around a red candle. Put the candle in a darkened room in the middle of a table. Write what it is you want on a piece of paper with a quill pen dipped in black ink. Chant the following as you write:

What I want I write here. Please take my dream and bring it near. What I want Is What I should get. Let all my dreams Now be met.

Now take the paper and fold it in a square of four creases. hold it over the candle with a pair of tweezers and let it burn. Picture yourself with your wish fulfilled as you burn the paper send waves of love at the image you conjure of your self. There is only one catch for this spell, be careful what you ask for.

DIVINE MONEY SPELLS
Dragonstar ~ William Oribello

GOOD LUCK SPELL FOR LOTTERY

For success in the lottery and other games of chance, say these words when the moon is full:

Lady of luck come out of your hidden course,
bless your light upon me as the light of the moon
shines above and in the light of luck will be blessed I
when the moon is next to be full.

MONEY IN MY POCKET

This is a fast and fun spell you can drum, clap, sing, chant, whenever you get worried about money. Children love this one as well.

Money in my pocket
and money in my hand
money in my home
and money in my bank

Money streams towards me
and makes its home with me
its easy and its wonderful
as counting 1-2-3!

And...

There's money in my pocket
and money in my hand,
money in my home
and money in my bank.

DIVINE MONEY SPELLS
Dragonstar ~ William Oribello

Wherever I shall go
and whatever I may do
I clearly state the fact
its true and it is so!

Repeat this spell as often as you like.

THE CHARGE OF JUPITER

You will need: one green candle and a photo of the person who owes you money. This is to be used for visualization if needed.

The Projective Hand is the hand that is normally used for manual activities such as writing, peeling apples and dialing telephones is symbolically thought to be the point at which personal power is visualized as streaming from the body. In ritual, personal power is visualized streaming out of the palm or fingers of the hand for various magical goals. This is also the hand in which tools such as the Athame and wand are held. Ambidextrous persons simply chose which hand to utilize for this purpose.

Hold the candle in your projective hand and visualize the money re-manifesting in you life. Remember, never visualize the process of getting the money, visualize receiving the money from the one who owes it to you.

Recite the following:

I charge you by Jupiter,
I charge you by the Earth, I charge you Sun, Moon,
and Stars: Bring back my money to me, Prosperity.
Money to me, Prosperity. Money to me, Prosperity.

DIVINE MONEY SPELLS
Dragonstar ~ William Oribello

Place the candle in its holder. Light it and sit or stand before it watching the flame transform the wax into a liquid. Visualize the candle releasing the energies that you've placed within it. Sense it sending out power to bring the return of your money into manifestation. Let the candle burn down to its end, or, allow it to burn for 4, 8, or 16 minutes daily until your need manifests.

SPELL TO MEET EXISTING NEEDS

This spell helps bring money to meet existing needs. You need to be precise as to how much money you need, and for what reason you want it for. This is what to focus on.

At the start of your day write down, type or print from your computer how much money you need, and what you want it for. Next, draw a line around that statement.

Example: I need $500 to pay the bills.

Or: I want $1,000 to buy a new or used car.

Fold the paper in half and in half again, and carry it with you during the day, for at least 12 hours. Reread the paper, several times, during the day.

When the night comes, go into your bedroom, or ritual room, and light a new white candle.

Open the paper you have been carrying, and reread the message that you wrote, one more time. Say these words, three times:

From beyond this candle light,
The powers that rule over money come,
To bring to me this needed sum,
Aided by a cosmic name,
Because I burn this sacred flame.

31

Tear up the paper, and discard it in a wastebasket. Repeat, each night, for seven days, or until the money comes. This spell is very powerful, and effective, when you correctly follow the instructions.

MONEY DOUBLING SPELL

This spells helps double any denomination of cash paper money that you have.

First find some almost new cash paper money, in the largest denomination possible. The twenty or fifty dollar bill is good.

Place this in a white envelope and seal it. Fold the envelope and say once, every day, for about seven days:

Occult powers to me shall bring,
The way to double this sum.
Hear me, thou cherubim which sing,
Quickly, and softly come.

Hold the envelope up, and pretend that it has become heavier. Keep the envelope in your bedroom. After you receive more money, open the envelope and either spend, or deposit the money that was in the envelope.

BRING MONEY FOR SOMEONE ELSE

A very simple spell is to take a photograph of the person (if you don't have one, carefully write out their full name on a piece of paper); also find whatever you have in the way of coins and notes in your purse or about your house.

Put four candles in a square and the photo in the middle.

Gather the money in both hands. Hold it over the photo. Take three deep breaths and concentrate on the person.

Now rain all the money on the photo and say:
From above, from below
money will now come to you
money rains, and money flows
Its my will and it is so.

Leave the money on the photo overnight or until the candles have burned right down (if you start with smaller candles or tealights, that's safer and faster).

Then wrap up what's left of the candles, one coin, one note and the photograph; tie it in a bundle of tissue paper with green string and put it in a safe place.

When the person had their money problems solved, you can take back the coin and note and throw the rest away because the spell is done.

TAROT SPELL FOR SUCCESSFUL HOME BUSINESS

From a Tarot deck you will need the following cards: Ace of Wands - III of Wands - IV of Sands - IX of Pentacles

Ritual: Lay out the IV of Wands and visualize your business starting with an abundance of customers and happy times.

Next, lay out the Ace of Wands - visualizing pouring your energy in to this enterprise - if you have any tools of your trade, handle them as you do so.

Now l ay out the III of Wands, picture a typical working day at your new company answering the phone -all the business you need and want, picture the little things that make up a typical business day.

Lay out the IX of Pentacles...envision the ultimate security you have achieved thru this business and the satisfaction you have gained. Visualize yourself smiling and content. Say the following as you lay out the final card:

With this spell I bring power to my resolve I start my own business I enjoy the advantages and benefits of making my home my place of business as I start this business not only do I cast this spell but I also work unceasingly to make my business a success. I have chosen work I enjoy and business will be good. As I cast this spell - I cast forth my will - I charge this spell to make word of my product spread. Let those who use my product be attracted to me and see what I have to offer. In this way the ends I desire shall be achieved comfort security and contentment. So be it.

Repeat this spell for four days and then hold off for four days. Repeat the same sequence of days four times. You should see an increase in business at the end of the sequence.

CHAPTER THREE – CANDLE MAGICK SPELLS

One of the most popular and easiest forms of Magick is candle burning. Its popularity is due to the fact that candle Magick is relatively easy to perform, and employs little ritual and few ceremonial artifacts. The theatrical props of candle Magick can be purchased at any department store and its rituals can be practiced in any quiet room of the house.

Most of us have experienced candle Magick on our birthdays, blowing out the candles on our birthday cakes and making a wish is pure candle Magick. This childhood custom is based on the three magickal principles of concentration, will power and visualization. In simple terms, the child who wants his wish to come true has to concentrate (blow out the candles), visualize the end result (make a wish) and hope that it will come true (will power).

The size and shape of the candles you use isn't important, although ornate, extra large or unusually shaped candles usually are suitable. The reason for this is that such candles may create distractions when the practitioner wants to concentrate on the important work in hand.

Most candle-users prefer to use candles of standard or uniform size if possible. Those which are sold in different colors for home use are perfect for candle Magick.

Candles used for any type of magickal invocation should be pristine. Under no circumstances use a candle which has already adorned a dinner table or been used as a bedroom candle or nightlight. The reason is that vibrations picked up by secondhand materials or equipment may disturb your workings and negate their effectiveness.

Some candle-users who are artistically inclined prefer to make their own candles for magickal use. This is a very practical exercise because not only does it impregnate the candle with your own personal vibrations, but the mere act of making your own candle is magickally potent. Craft shops which sell candle making supplies can also provide do-it-yourself books explaining the technicalities of the art to the beginner.

Once you have purchased or made your ritual candle, it has to be oiled or "dressed" before burning. Fragrance is an extremely useful tool. It "sets the mood" for your ritual, and goes a long way in bringing about your desired magickal intention.

The purpose of dressing the candle is to establish a psychic link between it and the magician through a primal sensory experience. By physically touching the candle during the dressing procedure, you are charging it with your own personal vibrations and also concentrating the desire of your will directly into the wax. The candle will become an extension of the magician's mental power and life energy.

When you dress a candle for magickal use, imagine that it is a psychic magnet with a north and a south pole. Rub the oil into the candle beginning at the top or north end and work downwards to the half-way point. Always brush in the same direction downwards. This process is then repeated by beginning at the bottom or south end and working up to the middle.

The best type of oils to use for dressing candles are natural ones which can be obtained quite easily. Some occult suppliers will provide candle Magick oils with exotic names. If the practitioner does not want to use these, he can select suitable oils or perfumes from his own sources. The oil soluble perfumes sold by craft shops for inclusion in homemade candles can be successfully used.

There are any number of popular oils that are commonly used in Magick. Some have a long history of use due to their commonly accepted magickal attributes. Don't be afraid to experiment with different fragrances from oils and incense. Your personal involvement in choosing the right oils is what is important to achieve the proper results.

DIVINE MONEY SPELLS
Dragonstar ~ William Oribello

Some excellent oils for Divine Money Spells are: Bayberry, Bergamot, Cedarwood, Cinnamon, Ginger, Honeysuckle, Jasmine, Musk, Orange, Strawberry, and Violet.

BASIC CANDLE MAGICK

Basic candle Magick deals only with two colors, white and black. Envision the white candle as the waxing to full moon and the black candle as the waning to new moon. For any calling purposes, use the white candle. For any banishing purposes, use the black candle.

Over the years the use of colored candles has gained in popularity. However, purists of candle Magick are insistent that the uses of colored candles are simply not necessary. There is also debate on whether or not colored candles serve more as a distraction rather then help the Magick. Nevertheless, the use of colored candles is widely established. Each color supposedly has its own magickal significance.

For Divine Money Spells you can never go wrong with using green candles to attract money and prosperity. However, colors such as Gold, Orange and Purple are also excellent choices to assist in your candle Magick rituals.

The use of colored candles for Divine Money Spells is a splendid way to invoke the hidden energies of Creation. The colors you use can also have a deeper personal significance. This is encouraged since a more intimate connection with the candles will always achieve better results.

Feel free to experiment with different colors. Always remember to write down the types of success you have with different colors. That way, when you are trying to achieve a certain goal, you can go back and check your notes.

The simplest form of candle Magick is to write down the objective of your ritual on a virgin piece of paper. You can also use color paper which matches the color of the candle.

DIVINE MONEY SPELLS
Dragonstar ~ William Oribello

Write your petition on the paper. As you write down what you want to accomplish through candle Magick, visualize your dream coming true. When you have completed writing down your petition, carefully fold up the paper in a deliberately slow fashion. Place the end of the folded paper in the candle flame and set light to it. As you does this concentrate once more on what you want from life.

I don't have to tell you to be extremely careful when you do this last part. Make sure that you are in a safe place and have a safe, fireproof container to place your burning petition. After all, it would not do you any good to burn your house down when trying to draw in a little folding cash.

When you have completed your ritual, allow the candle to completely burn down. You do not need to stay with the candle after the ritual, but make sure that is safe and that hot wax will not cause damage or fire.

Never re-use a candle used for any magickal ritual. A candle should only be used in one ritual and then allowed to burn away or be disposed of afterwards.

A note about putting out candles, do not blow out a candle. Snuff it out. The only time you would blow out a magickal candle is when you need an emergency stop. Finalizing the energy in such a way will cause a psychic backlash, so be prepared.

Now that you are ready to try your first candle Magick spell, make sure you have everything you need to insure a successful invocation. Before performing any kind of magickal works, be sure that you have the consent of anyone that will be involved. All Magick, even candle Magick, comes back on the petitioner three fold, so it is important to check into your motives before beginning any sort of spell.

Casting spells uses personal energy, so be sure that your mind is not cluttered and that you are not tired, as Magick often tires the practitioner. Light some incense...this enables

DIVINE MONEY SPELLS
Dragonstar ~ William Oribello

the practitioner to attune to his psychic mind, and contact his personal energies. A good night's sleep before any candle Magick will aid in using your energy to its fullest.

The next thing you will want to do is anoint your candle with oil. Remember, anointing is done by rubbing the candle in the upward motion, starting in the middle of your candle. Only rub in that direction, all the while concentrating on what you are trying to accomplish...your intention is to rub that goal into the candle. Then, starting in the middle again, rub the candle downward. Continue to rub the candle in this direction, concentrating on your goal. When you feel that the candle is successfully oiled, consider it blessed.

Now is the time to light the candle. Keep your goal firmly in mind. Visualize your goal. See your goal in the fire. Continue to gaze into the fire, visualizing strongly, until you are too tired to continue. You may then leave your flame.

It is important to let your candle burn all the way out. This allows the energy that you infused into the candle to be completely released. When the spell is complete if you are trying to invoke something cast the ashes to the wind. If you are banishing, throw the remains in the garbage.

If for some reason you need to reverse a candle Magick spell, gather all melted wax, burned incense, recopy all requests used in the spell you want to reverse or stop.

Find yourself a gray candle and some reversing oil and incense. Cedar is good for both a reversing oil and incense.

On a waning Moon cast a circle of white protective light around yourself and the candle. Place the candle in the middle of your alter. A small table or desktop can be used. Place all the items from the spell you want to reverse or stop around the gray candle and say:

These things have I wrought will now cease to exist.
Go back the way you have begun, cease now and

desist. With harm to none and no alarm the energies dissipate. Return all things now as they were. I relinquish them to fate.

Light the candle and allow it to burn down.

A QUICK CANDLE MONEY SPELL

If you owe money take a green candle and anoint it with cinnamon oil. Take a piece of paper and write on it the amount of money that you owe and who it is for.

You will need a candle that can burn for seven days. Place the paper under the candle. Hold your hands over the candle and say:

This candle burns to light the way
for the money I need to pay this bill
in a way that harms no one.

Light the candle and burn patchouli incense. Meditate for about five minutes as the candle burns. Visualize yourself writing the check or purchasing the money order for this bill and putting it in the mail.

Burn the candle every day around the same time for seven days and 15 minutes at a time. Also, burn patchouli incense every day with the candle. On the last day, burn the paper with the flame from the candle and let the candle burn completely out.

DIVINE MONEY SPELLS
Dragonstar ~ William Oribello

SPELL TO GET WHAT YOU WANT

All you need are the three basic Magick necessities, need, emotion, and knowledge. Light a candle and concentrate on only what you need. Say the following:

I give, because I'm generous. I take because I ask.
What I well deserve is what I will get.
I deserve (whatever you need) I need (whatever you need)
I will get (whatever you need) so be it, and so it is.

Allow the candle to burn out on its own and repeat once a day for three days.

CANDLE AND PENNY SPELL

An extremely simple yet effective spell for obtaining fast money when needed is the following: On a Friday during the Waxing Moon anoint a green candle with an appropriate money-drawing oil, such as Patchouly, Jasmine, or Cinnamon. Take the candle and place in a holder. Place a brand new shiny penny in front of the holder, and then surround the holder with three green aventurine gemstones. Repeat the following chant three times:

Money, money come to me,
$100 is what I need.
With harm to none and help to many,
multiply now this shiny penny!

DIVINE MONEY SPELLS
Dragonstar ~ William Oribello

Now light your candle and gaze into its flame, strongly visualizing the needed money coming to you. Continue with this visualization for as long as possible. After the candle has burned down completely, bury any remaining wax on your property and carry the penny with you to reinforce your magickal intention.

A SILVER SPELL

Situate a small bowl of any material in a place of prominence in your home, somewhere you pass by every day. Each day for seven days put one dime in the bowl. Next, obtain a green candle, any shape or kind.

Before you begin, fix in your mind the idea that you are a prosperous person. See money as being no problem. Imagine money coming to you, as you need it.

Place the bowl of dimes, the candle and a candle holder on a flat surface. Hold the candles in your hands and feel the power of money. Feel the avenues that open to you when you have it. Sense the energy within money which we as human beings have given to it. Place the candle in the holder.

Pour the seven dimes into your left hand. You will create a circle surrounding the candles with the dimes. Place the first dime directly before the candle. As you place it say these or similar words:

Money flow, money shine,
Money grow, Money mine.

Repeat this six more times until you've created a circle around the candle with seven gleaming dimes.

DIVINE MONEY SPELLS
Dragonstar ~ William Oribello

As you say the words and place the dimes, know that you are not just reciting and fooling around with pieces of metal. You're working with power, that which we've given money as well as that which is within yourself. Words too have energy, as does the breath on which they ride.

When you have completed this, light the candle and visualize the energy within the flame becoming one with your wish for money. See the power of money flowing out from the seven dimes up to the candle's flames and then out to the atmosphere.

Settle down before the glowing candle and money. Sense the feeling of money in your life. Visualize a life with money to spare, a life in which bills are quickly paid and money will never again be a problem.

See yourself wisely spending money, investing it for your future needs. See money as an unavoidable and beautiful aspect of your life. Kill off any thoughts of debt, of taxes, of doubt that you can achieve this change. Simply see what will be. See what is to be real.

After ten minutes or so, leave the area. Let the candle burn itself out in the holder. Afterward, collect the dimes, place them back in the bowl, and "feed" it a few coins every day from then on. Money will come to you.

BECOME A PROSPERITY MAGNET

You will need one green candle, a candle holder and a lighter. If you really want to be in sync with natural energies, do this visualization during the waxing moon i.e. during the two weeks when the Moon is increasing in light, from New to Full.

Close your eyes and breathe slowly, deeply and rhythmically until you feel completely relaxed. Imagine yourself surrounded by white light, enclosed in a bright bubble of energy or otherwise protected from harm. If it makes you more comfortable call upon the Creator, your personal guardian angel, spirit guide, or patron saint to be with you in this work.

Begin to visualize money flowing into your life. You don't have to imagine how this is going to happen. In your mind's eye see dollar bills or silver dollars or whatever signifies money to you being blown towards you from above and from all directions. What does it feel like to have this money, to have the ability to pay all your bills or the freedom to buy what you most want? Try to both mentally picture this as clearly as you can and feel it emotionally.

Now pick up the candle and hold it tightly in your hands until you feel your pulse throbbing beneath your fingers. Your energy and the prosperous energies of the universe symbolized by the green candle are merging together. You are becoming a prosperity magnet. Affirm your desire (to yourself or out loud). For example:

Money streams continuously into my life,
with harm towards none.

Continue visualizing and chanting as you place the candle in the holder and light it. Cup your hands around the flame, feeling its warmth and energy. Put the candle in a safe place and let it burn down naturally.

DIVINE MONEY SPELLS
Dragonstar ~ William Oribello

MONEY, MONEY, COME TO ME...

Using candle Magick to draw money can be a very powerful spell. Great care must be taken whenever doing any kind of drawing Magick, due to the possibility that your spell could accidentally harm someone close to you. Always make sure you include in your ritual the command that your request will cause no harm or misfortune.

To work this candle spell you will need seven purple candles. Anoint each candle with ginger, honeysuckle, or jasmine oil. With a new straight pin, carve on each candle your first name, and the word "MONEY." Visualize yourself receiving money through a new job, a pay raise, winning a contest. Never visualize cash just appearing to you, generally because that money will have to come from someone else, usually a poor, unfortunate relative. Light all seven candles while saying with each candle:

Money, Money, Come to Me.

Allow each candle to burn out and gather up the remains and bury close by.

MONEY THREE TIMES THREE

Gather together and place on your altar: altar cloth, green candle, crisp dollar bill, favorite incense, spring water, and a small magnet.

Draw your circle around your sacred space, and raise your arms to the universe, taking a deep breath.

DIVINE MONEY SPELLS
Dragonstar ~ William Oribello

Light the candle and the incense, and visualize yourself as a prosperous, wealthy person, let your thoughts flow imagining the life you live with enormous wealth.

First, immerse the dollar bill in the spring water, then wave the dollar bill back and forth through the smoke of the burning incense, and recite:

This candle burns to light the way
Money, money come to me
Harming no one else along the way
Bring me money three times three.

Do this as many times as you see fit, usually three times will suffice. As you do this, continue to visualize your new, prosperous life.

Now wrap the dollar bill around the magnet and carry it with you at all times in your pocket, and keep your mind focused on the prosperity that is coming your way. In no time you'll find unexpected bits of money coming to you.

When you're finished, remember to open the circle, and let the candle and incense burn out.

THE NINE DAY MONEY SPELL

This spell is similar to the last spell and can be done at any time, but preferably at the same time each day or night. You will need a green candle and a white candle. The green candle represents the money, and the white candle represents you. You will also need one green tourmaline, or a quartz crystal that you have charge with money vibrations.

DIVINE MONEY SPELLS
Dragonstar ~ William Oribello

Make sure you anoint the candles with oil first, thinking of your desire for money to come to you. Set the candles on a table nine inches apart with your gemstone placed between them. After doing this say out loud:

Money, money come to me
In abundance three times three
May I be enriched in the best of ways
Harming none on its way
This I accept, so it be
Bring me money three times three!

Repeat this spell for nine days. Each day move the white candle one inch closer to the green candle. When the candles touch the crystal, your spell is finished. Make sure you visualize the money pouring in from the universe. The crystal can now be recharged for future use.

MONEY SPELL BY THE LIGHT OF THE FULL MOON

Here is an old Celtic spell using one small white candle and one green-colored stone of your choice. Fill a clear glass with fresh rain water and drop your gemstone and a silver coin into it. Position the glass so that the light from the moon shines into the water. Gently sweep your hands just above the surface, symbolically gathering the moon's silver. While doing this say the following chant:

Lovely Lady of the Moon, bring to me your
wealth right soon. Fill my hands with silver
and gold. All you give, my purse can hold.

DIVINE MONEY SPELLS
Dragonstar ~ William Oribello

Repeat this three times. When finished, pour the water upon the earth and visualize money and success growing out of the ground like grain in a summer's field.

Take the green gemstone and store it in a safe, dark place until the next full moon. If this spell does not work in the first month, repeat once more with the same stone, but a fresh silver coin. The stone can be saved and recharged for future use.

TO GET WHAT YOU WANT

Take a horseshoe and put it around a red candle. Place the candle in a darkened room in the middle of a table. Write what it is you want on a piece of paper with a quill pen dipped in black ink. Chant the following as you write.

What I want I write here.
Please take my dream and bring it near.
What I want is what I should get.
Let all my dreams now be met.

Now take the paper and fold it in a square of four creases. Hold it over the candle with a pair of tweezers and let it burn. Picture yourself with your wish fulfilled as you burn the paper, sending waves of love, happiness and contentment at the image you conjure of yourself.

DIVINE MONEY SPELLS
Dragonstar ~ William Oribello

HOW TO ATTRACT SUCCESS TO YOUR BUSINESS

All of the measures below are calculated to draw customers, and thusly success, to you and your business.

In New Orleans it is believed that Saint Peter governs business because he carries keys. Get up early in the morning and light a white candle to Saint Peter. Then mix green herbs into a bucket of water...especially parsley and thyme.

Begin mopping the floor from the front of your business toward the back, moving backwards as you go. When you reach the back of your business, burn some green incense.

Get up early and burn mixture of sulfur and sugar and money drawing incense. As the sun rises, look to the east and pray for customers to be drawn to you.

Go to the graveyard and get nine handfuls of dirt. Back home, mix it with brimstone, sulfur, red pepper, and salt. Burn the mixture and pray for success in business.

PATHWAY TO SUCCESS SPELL

This spell is to be done between 8pm to 9pm under a waxing moon and will give you a short lived window of opportunity to find the path to succeed in attaining that which you desire.

You will need: Sandalwood Incense, Anise Oil, Orange candle (for success), Red candle (for action), Orange cloth, Piece of paper and a Pen.

DIVINE MONEY SPELLS

Dragonstar ~ William Oribello

Lay out the orange cloth. Inscribe your desired success on the orange candle and your name and birthdate on the red candle. Anoint both with the Anise oil.

When your incense is smoldering and the candles lit, close your eyes and envision yourself attaining your goal. Keeping your eyes closed, take the pen and hold it in your hand over the piece of paper. You may feel warmness and tingling in your arm – do not be alarmed.

Now, keep your eyes closed and concentrate as one of two things will occur: your arm may begin to wander and move making writings on the paper (automatic writing) or you will be given a very clear plan of action to write down manually.

Either through the automatic writing or through direct inspiration, you will be shown the way to success in that which you endeavor to achieve. As with any spell, this will not work if you are not serious about it.

POSITIVE ACTION SPELL

To be done under the full moon with one red candle and Musk oil. Inscribe your name or the phrase "Action be swift" on the red candle and anoint with the Musk oil. Situate yourself with the moon shining on your altar or work area if possible. (If this is not possible, just visualize the moon.)

Place the candle on your altar or work area and light. Speak the following words out loud or silently:

Tonight the moon, Tomorrow the sun.
Let power build till my will be done.

DIVINE MONEY SPELLS
Dragonstar ~ William Oribello

Candle burn down, to send my desire
Action be swift as the flames of this fire

Let the candle burn down completely, preferably in sight of the full moon.

BANISH POVERTY

The moon should be dark or waning. You should perform this on a Saturday. Light a white candle and take seven sheets of toilet paper and write: "I banish poverty" On each sheet. Flush them all down the toilet saying: *I banish poverty.* With each one. Do this every day from the full moon to the dark moon.

A WISH SPELL

Although this is not specifically a money spell, it is often used as such.

On the night of the new moon, write your wish on a clean piece of paper. Light a white candle and turn off all lights. Think about the fulfillment of your wish for several minutes then say:

As I sleep tonight may
the divine power of spiritual

DIVINE MONEY SPELLS
Dragonstar ~ William Oribello

love and light grant my wish

Then think about your wish as you burn the paper in the votive candle. Repeat this ritual at the same time on 12 consecutive nights. If you miss a night begin spell from day one.

DIVINE GUARDIAN ANGEL SPELL

Place three candles surrounded by sugar on a plate at the highest point in your home. Light the candles and ask for three wishes to the three guardian angels Rafael, Michael and Gabriel. One wish for success, one wish for prosperity and one impossible wish. Repeat this spell for three days. If your wishes come through, publish your thanks to your guardian angels in the classified ads in the local newspaper.

NONSENSE WORDS SPELL

With a green marker or crayon, draw a money symbol ($) on a piece of paper. Set atop of it a green candle and say this charm:

Flibberty, gibberty, flasky flum,
Calafa, tarada, wagra wum.
Hooky, maroosky, whatever's the sum,
Heigho! Presto! Money come!

DIVINE MONEY SPELLS
Dragonstar ~ William Oribello

Allow the candle to burn itself out, or allow the candle to burn each night for a week.

The paper is then to be folded in half four times and tied with a green string. This charm is to be carried with you for a week.

CANDLE AND CLOVES

Rub a small green candle with powdered cloves. Put it in a holder and set it on top of a new dollar bill.

On a Thursday afternoon, three hours after sunset, light the candle and let it burn until it burns out.

The next day bury the candle stub; rub the bill with powdered cloves and place it in a safe place in your home. You will never want nor need.

CARVING MAGICKAL SYMBOLS SPELL

A green candle would work, but use a red candle in conjunction with it, as red will help speed up the Magick. Start by cleaning the candle, simply take a paper towel or rag, and wipe from the middle of the candle, to the top, away from you. Turn the candle clockwise and do the same thing from the middle to the end, away from you.

DIVINE MONEY SPELLS
Dragonstar ~ William Oribello

Then carve the candle, all the while concentrating on your objective, namely getting money, in a speedy fashion. You can carve money signs ($) and any other symbols you feel work for you.

After carving, anoint the candle, again concentrating on your purpose. Use whatever essential oil you like, cinnamon or sandalwood are always good choices, and circle the top of the candle clockwise. Then, starting at the top of the candle, pulling the strokes toward you (because you want the money to come to you), with the oil. Circle the bottom of the candle clockwise with oil also.

You only need a few drops of oil for the anointing. If any oil is left on your fingers you can make a pentagram on your forehead, and over your heart, thanking the Creator and asking to grant your magickal request. When done, take a drop of honey and put it on the bottom of the candle, as an offering to the Creator, and lick the remainder off your finger.

Light the candle, and leave it burn. If you have to go out, put the candle in your kitchen sink, in a container with sand in it (to absorb the heat). If you must extinguish the candle, don't blow it out (it'll scatter the energy), wave or snuff it out.

When you re-light it, concentrate again on your purpose of attracting money with no harm to others.

55

DIVINE MONEY SPELLS
Dragonstar ~ William Oribello

CANDLE BURNING MAGICK AND THE PSALMS

This section of candle burning with the Psalms combines a presentation of the magickal virtues within a section of the 150 Psalms of the Holy Bible, and an unusual method of invoking the Divine Names of Power in order to gain money, success and prosperity.

In order to gain the greatest benefit from this section, the reader is encouraged to proceed in the following manner. First, a practitioner of this work must keep his or her activities confidential. The reason for this is obvious when we realize that not all people believe in this work. One thing the practitioner does not need is to be discouraged by those who think negatively. Cane who seeks to improve oneself by these methods must practice with friends of like mind, and be silent about it while in the presence of those who do not believe.

The practitioner must also approach this work with confidence that the Higher Power, that which we call God the Creator, will reward every sincere effort. Divine Mind, or God, does not accept only those of a formal religious persuasion, but all who have a sincere heart, regardless of formal religious affiliation or the lack of it, for the highest religion is to search for truth wherever we are. You are the living Temple of God, and the whole universe is your kingdom.

Finally, let the practitioner of this sacred art maintain a positive mental attitude. Do not try too hard to believe: simply perform your work in a relaxed condition, knowing that you are doing something of value that will bring positive results into your life. Whenever you finish your work, go about your daily routine with a calm attitude of expectancy – until the next session. Constant effort with simple faith is the path to success in any type of effort.

May your every effort be crowned with abundant success, as you embark on your journey into the realm of Divine Money Spells using candles and the Psalms.

DIVINE MONEY SPELLS
Dragonstar ~ William Oribello

PREPARING A CANDLE TO ATTRACT

When you wish to attract a certain thing into your life such as money, success and prosperity, you must prepare the candle by applying oil to it as you hold a mental picture of your desire. As was discussed earlier in this chapter, some practitioners use olive oil; others use special purpose oil for anointing candles, which can be obtained from spiritual/occult supply stores. Remember, at one time there were no stores to buy magickal oils and products, a practitioner had to make their own oils out of whatever was available to them. So don't worry if you can't find specialty oils, whatever method you feel works best for you is the correct method.

To anoint a candle to attract, the practitioner must apply some oil to the bottom of the candle on one side, then rub upward and stop at the center. Then one applies oil to the top of the candle, rub downward and stop at the same center spot.

It is best to use only one candle for each purpose. Once you prepare a candle for a special purpose, do not use that candle for any other reason.

The next rule is that you must burn the candle only while you are performing the chosen prayer ritual from this section. When you have finished, extinguish the flame, allow to cool and then put the candle away until your next session for the same purpose.

It is alright to ritual for several different things at once, but not in the same session. For example, you can ritual for a financial blessing, and when you have finished, put that candle away. Then you can begin working with the next candle for another purpose.

The last rule is that when your candle has burned down to a stub, you should dispose of it properly. Some practitioners of this art wrap the leftover wax in a piece of cloth and bury it. Others prefer to throw it into running water. You may select the method that suits you.

DIVINE MONEY SPELLS
Dragonstar ~ William Oribello

THE DIVINE NAMES OF POWER

The Creator has many names, each having a virtue to channel Divine Power into a life or situation when used in a correct manner.

The Divine Names of Power, as they are commonly known, are hidden within the scriptures. They were discovered by the technique known as Gematria that is often used by mystics to find the hidden within the obvious. This is part of the mystical system known as the Kabalah, said to have been communicated to wise men by Divine Revelation.

Divine Names, when written or spoken in a certain way, release an awesome power for great accomplishments. Many of the Divine Names are hidden within the Psalms and this accounts for their potential as tools for magickal accomplishments.

In order to use the Divine Names correctly for these Divine Money Spells you must carve the Sacred Name into the candle. Some practitioners use a knife or letter opener to carve the Divine Name. Others use a special talisman called the Glorious Sword, or the Sword of St. Michael.

It is best not to repeat the Divine Names out loud, unless the practitioner is able to pronounce them in the Hebrew language correctly. To carve the Divine Names of Power on candles is a technique of silent invocation to the power within that name, and this will be the special method that you will use for the work in this book.

The Biblical Book of Psalms has long been regarded as a book of personal power. This is because there are Divine Names and words of power hidden within its passages, as in all sacred writings.

Since the fall of man, Angelic Beings have communicated to the human race certain formulas by which humanity could regain the lost power of its original state. This body of teaching has been called the Secret Doctrine, the Kabalah, and by other terms.

This knowledge was mastered by the Prophet Moses, and handed down from generation to generation. It was expressed in a beautiful form by the author of the Psalms, generally believed to be King David.

Many practitioners of the Secret Wisdom use the Psalms as a tool to improve their condition in life, according to techniques handed down through the ages. There are traditional uses for the Psalms that have been given for the benefit of humankind. However, in this book the student will discover a slight variation of some of the older methods, in accordance with the techniques of triple power. These have been tested by the author with favorable results. Use the Bible you have at home to find the Psalms you need. There is no wrong or right Bible, whichever version you feel most comfortable with is the right one for you.

A practitioner of Divine Money Spells must first prepare the candle as described earlier. The next step is to carve the Divine name of the selected Psalm on the candle. The practitioner must then light the candle and begin their ritual. We have selected only the Psalms that deal with money, success and prosperity for this book. The first step of the ritual is to repeat the prescribed Psalm out loud. What follows should be a sincere prayer, asking for the desired help in accomplishing your special purpose. You should always pray in your own words, for then the prayer will be from the heart. Finally one should remain in silent meditation on desired results for a few moments before closing the ritual.

As you select the various rituals to improve your condition, you must do so with a feeling of expectancy and an attitude of faith, that you will receive the desired help from Higher Realms. When you complete your session, do not think too much about it or worry as to how your help will come. Just be at ease, trying to be aware of opportunities that may arise in your daily life.

DIVINE MONEY SPELLS
Dragonstar ~ William Oribello

Repeat a ritual for a specific purpose as often as possible, until you see the desired results. Keep a positive mental attitude, and speak in a more positive manner. As you follow these instructions, you will discover, as many have, that the faithful and sincere use of the Psalms will bless your life with a greater power and harmony with God and all other beings.

Psalm 4
To have good luck with money and success.

Prepare a green candle to attract. The Divine Name is "JIHEJE".

Note: For good luck with money and success, this Psalm, along with a sincere prayer is to be repeated three times before sunrise. You should continue this until you see a change in your condition.

Psalm 8
To win favor with all people in business transactions.

Prepare a green candle to attract. The Divine Name is "RECHMIAL".

Note: This Psalm, along with a sincere prayer is to be repeated after sundown, for three evenings in succession.

DIVINE MONEY SPELLS
Dragonstar ~ William Oribello

Psalm 32
To receive Divine Grace with prosperity.

Prepare a purple candle to attract. The Divine Name is "I.H.V.H.".

Psalm 57
To attract more good fortune with money.

Prepare a green candle to attract. The Divine Name is "CHAT".

Psalm 65
To have good fortune when seeking a better job.

Prepare a green candle to attract. The Divine Name is **"JAK"**.

Psalms 96 & 97
To bring money and good fortune to your family.

Prepare a green candle to attract. The Divine Name is **"JAH"**.

Note: Both of these Psalms should be used, followed by sincere prayer.

Psalm 108
To be successful and prosperous at home and work.

Prepare a green candle to attract. The Divine Name is **"VI"**.

DIVINE MONEY SPELLS
Dragonstar ~ William Oribello

Psalm 114
To find the perfect job.

Prepare a green candle to attract. The Divine Name is "AHA".

Psalm 119 - Verses 113 through 120.
To receive money in times of need.

Prepare a purple candle to attract. The Divine Name is "SAMECH".

Psalm 119 - verses 137 through 144.
To receive intuitive guidance when making an important decision concerning money.

Prepare a blue candle to attract. The Divine Name is "TZADDI".

Psalm 120
For a successful outcome concerning debt and other money troubles.

Prepare a purple candle to attract. The Divine Name is "I.H.V.H.".

Psalm 134
To gain more knowledge about money and success.

Prepare a purple candle to attract. The Divine Name is "I.H.V.H.".

DIVINE MONEY SPELLS
Dragonstar ~ William Oribello

Psalm 135
To experience God.

Prepare a purple candle to attract. The Divine Name is
"I.H.V.H.".

Psalm 150
To turn money woes into success.

Prepare a red candle to attract. The Divine Name is
"I.H.V.H.".

Novenas for Special Intents

There are some other methods, besides the Psalms, to draw in money and prosperity by using candles and prayers. There are Seven Day Novena Candles, candles, in glass, which are designed to burn for seven consecutive days. When using these candles, each day, for seven days, one is pray before the Novena candle the prayer(s) for that saint and intent. Usually the prayer(s) are printed on the glass container. It is best to say the novena prayer(s) at the same time each day.

When praying your novena, make the sign of the cross (†) and say "† In the Name of the Father, The Son, and The Hoy Spirit. † Amen.", before and after your novena prayer(s). When your petition is granted, be sure to keep any vow that you may have made and to publish a notice of thanksgiving.

Novena Prayers (To Use With Candles)

St. Barbara - Oh St. Barbara, As your last words to Christ Jesus, before the sword severed your head from your body, were that all those who invoked His Holy Name in memory of you, may find their sins forgotten on the Day of Judgment.

DIVINE MONEY SPELLS
Dragonstar ~ William Oribello

Help me in my tribulations, console me in my afflictions and intercede for me and for my family in our needs. Amen (Concentrate on your petition).

St. Expedito - Oh, Glorious Martyr and Protector, St. Expedito. We humbly ask to have fortune and prosperity for our country, that the sick get well, the guilty get pardoned, the just be preserved and those who abandon this valley of tears rest in the Light of The Lord and the souls of the dearly departed rest in peace. † (Mention your request). Amen

St. Jude - Most Holy Apostle, St. Jude, Faithful Servant and Friend of Jesus, pray for me who am so despaired in this hour of great need. Bring visible and speedy help for I promise you, O Blessed St. Jude to be ever mindful of this great favor. I will never cease to honor you as my most special, most powerful patron. Amen.

St. Lazarus - Oh Blessed Saint Lazarus, Patron of the Poor, I believe in you and call on your most holy spirit to grant me my favor. † In The Name Of The Father, The Son, and The Holy Spirit. I trust in your infinite goodness to intercede for me through Jesus Christ, Our Lord to grant me this petition (mention petition). Amen

Miraculous Mother - Oh, Miraculous Mother! With inspired confidence I call upon thee to extend thy merciful, loving kindness so that thy powers of perpetual help will protect me and assist me in my needs and difficulties. Please grant me my desire. Amen (Mention petition).

St. Michael - Oh Glorious Archangel St. Michael, watch over me during all my life. Defend me against the assaults of the demon. Assist me, especially at the hour of my death. Obtain for a favorable judgment and help me in all my needs. Amen.

Our Lady of Perpetual Help - Oh Mother of Perpetual Help, grant that I may ever invoke thy most powerful name. O purest Mary, O sweetest Mary, let thy name henceforth be ever on my lips. Delay not, O Blessed Lady, to help me whenever I call on thee. For in all my needs, in all my temptations, I shall never cease to call on thee, ever repeating thy sacred name, Mary, Mary. I will not be content with merely pronouncing thy name, but let my love for thee prompt me ever to hail thee, Mother Of Perpetual Help. Amen

Seven African Powers - Oh, Seven African Powers, who so close to Our Divine Savior, with great humility I kneel before you and implore your intercession before The Almighty. Hear my petition that I may glory in your powers to protect me, to help me and provide for my needs. Amen.

Working with the Saints

When asking the Saints to intercede on your behalf, it's most important to be sincere in your petition. Furthermore, it is not wise to ask for that which would be against that particular saint's nature or principals. It is most helpful to think through your request very thoroughly, perhaps even writing it down. Some saints are very appreciative of gifts, sometimes before you make your request, sometimes after and sometimes both.

Usually, one's prayers for intercession are accompanied by the burning of candles. Often, simple votive candles are sufficient, but 7-day novena candles of a color appropriate to the saint is even more effective. In addition, some saints have special oils for anointing their candle. Many people also wear the medal of a saint, particularly their patron saint, and carry a prayer card with the picture and prayer to the saint whose intercession is sought.

St. Anthony Of Padua - Find lost objects, works wonders.

St. Barbara - For love and friendship, conquer enemies.

St. Bernadette - For healing.

DIVINE MONEY SPELLS
Dragonstar ~ William Oribello

Our Lady of Charity - Protection of home, find lover, bring prosperity.

St. Christopher - Protection during travel.

St. Dymphna - For mental disorders, demonic possession.

St. Expeditus - Settle disputes, for pressing needs.

Our Lady of Guadalupe - Overcome fear, protection from jinxes.

St. Joseph - find job, sell or rent house.

St. Jude - For impossible situations.

St. Martin De Porres - For comfort, health, friends - good life.

St. Martin Caballero - Business, draw customers.

St. Michael - Overcome obstacles, defeat enemes, remove evil.

Miraculous Mother - Bring good things of life.

Our Lady of Perpetual Help - When in need of help.

St. Peter - Open roads, bring opportunities for success.

St. Ramond - Stop gossip and slander, silence enemies.

St. Raphael – "The Healer of God".

Sacred Heart Of Jesus - Blessed, peaceful life.

Sacred Heart Of Mary - Serenity and spiritual blessings.

Seven African Powers/Saints - All purpose, to solve problems.

DIVINE MONEY SPELLS
Dragonstar ~ William Oribello

CHAPTER FOUR – DIVINE CRYSTAL ENERGIES

Through the ages, Man has been attracted and incredibly drawn to the mystical beauty of crystals and gemstones. Archaeologists have discovered in graves and barrows excavated in Europe, the Middle East, Russia, and Africa beads, carvings, and jewelry of amber, jet, turquoise, lapis, garnet, carnelian, quartz, and other stones. It is believed that the carvings were probably amulets and talismans, used for protection and as reminders of religious rites.

Some of the discovered stones were carved in the shape of various animals, and were probably symbols of particular totems. Others were necklaces and other items of adornment. The value given to crystals in these various cultures is indicated by their presence in the graves; they were intended to go with the departed soul to help them in the next life.

Because of their unearthly beauty, shining stones were believed to have magickal powers. A magic wand tipped by a special gemstone could perform miracles. It was said that the rod Moses used to part the Dead Sea was encrusted with sacred gemstones. Gemstones were used in a vest adorned by priests of old to magnify their spiritual aura.

A good example of prehistoric reverence for crystals is the solar temple Newgrange. This ancient passage grave in the Boyne Valley of Ireland was built so that the sun would stream through the 70-foot-long entrance tunnel on the Winter Solstice. Its roof was originally covered with gleaming white quartz, to symbolize the White Goddess.

The Egyptians used crystals in their secret funeral ceremonies and in their magical cult practices. They assigned symbolic power meanings to them that gave the stones a value that exceeded their simple mineral origins. The meanings associated with them were for health, protection in life and the afterlife, and good fortune, just to name a few.

DIVINE MONEY SPELLS
Dragonstar ~ William Oribello

A hieroglyphic papyrus from the year 2000 B.C. documents a medical cure using a crystal, and several from the year 1500 B.C. have additional prescriptions. Lapis was considered to be a royal stone and its use was restricted for use only by the royal house. It was often pulverized and made into a poultice to be rubbed into the crown of the head. It was believed that as it dried it drew out all spiritual impurities.

The pharaohs often had their headdresses lined with malachite in the belief that it helped them to rule wisely. In powder form this stone was used for poor eyesight and inner vision. Many other stones were found in the tombs, including carnelian, turquoise, and tiger's eye.

According to Dragonstar legends, passed down for generations in ancient writings, the ancient Atlantean's used special crystals and gemstones for various functions in their daily lives. A number of crystals were shaped into inverted pyramids. These special stones had four to six sides and were infused with various shades of pink or rose which created a light beam that was excellent for surgery. These crystals were also excellent for soothing pain, particularly in the delicate areas of the brain, the eyes, the heart and reproductive organs.

Special gemstones that were gold or yellow would change colors to deeper hues in the presence of disease or bodily vibrational disorders. Ruby and purple stones helped cure emotional and spiritual problems. Black crystals were powerful protectors.

For general rejuvenation and a return of vitality the ancient Atlanteans periodically meditated 15 to 20 minutes inside a circle of six, eleven, twenty-two or twenty-four stones of different types, holding clear quartz in their hands, which acted as a control and focalizer.

The Atlanteans used the knowledge of the crystal refraction, amplification and storage. It is known that a beam of light directed intensely and focused specifically on certain series of facets in a gem will, when it exits from the reflective plane of the gem, be amplified rather than diminished. These amplified energies were broken down into a wide and sophisticated spectrum of color and sound frequencies. The Atlanteans used the spectrum of this energy for a specific purpose, much as one would use petroleum in terms of its various spectrum limitations for specific purposes.

The Atlantean crystals had the ability to transfer energy, to retain it, to maintain its intensity, to focus and transmit it over great distance to similar receivers as are equal or comparable to the transmitter.

These crystals were natural forms, but their growths were accelerated. Some clear quartz was grown to almost 25 feet high and 10 feet in diameter and had 12 sides and was used for storing and transmitting power.

All these various crystals received their power from a variety of sources, including the Sun, the Earth's energy grid system, or from each other. The larger stones, called Fire Crystals, were the central receiving and broadcasting stations, while others acted as receivers for individual cities, buildings, vehicles and homes. On a higher spiritual level, rooms made of crystals were places where the Initiates left their bodies in the Final Transcendence, often never to return.

The Atlanteans transmitted from energy from one pyramid to another. Depending on the tilt of the earth's axis at a particular time of the year one pyramid would function to intensify and transmit energies to other pyramids which would then act as receiving devices and would disperse energy as it was needed.

Though one may still find today a crystal that helps them link into the frequency of Atlantis – what it is doing is allowing themselves to connect with the grids that formed the Atlantean Program – or using the energies of the crystal – based on its shape and vibrational frequency to trigger a

DIVINE MONEY SPELLS
Dragonstar ~ William Oribello

memory in them about that civilization. These crystals may be found anywhere on the planet. They usually call to the person who links with them on the same frequency signature.

Many people living today are reincarnated Atlanteans who are here to help guide the planet through its next vibrational change. These special souls have a unique vibrational connection to the old crystal and gemstones.

THE DIVINE SPEAKS THROUGH CRYSTALS

Every culture has touched in some way, the spiritual energies of crystals and gemstones. Even the so-called primitive people of Neolithic and pre-historic times saw the connection between stones and the powers of nature. Many caves and antediluvian enclaves that have been excavated contained beautiful examples of gemstone carvings and amulets.

Crystals and gemstones are energetic keys that help unlock our potential and highest purposes for being. They can be stimulants to our creative and latent potentials, helping us to become "whole" as human beings. The use of gemstones and crystals as a focal point to the Divine can still be seen these days as rosaries for Christians and prayer beads for Muslims and Buddhists. These crystals on rosaries or prayer beads not only marked the number of prayers, chants or mantras but the belief is that rubbing and stroking the beads of crystals gave one a spiritual connection to God.

Crystals and gemstones were regarded as having great spiritual and emotional powers. Moonstone, for instance, was a sacred stone, and believed to arouse love and passion. Onyx, in contrast, was believed to help release the tie of old loves and allow for the heart to finally heal. The ruby, thought to be the dried blood of the gods, was known as the "king of precious stones."

DIVINE MONEY SPELLS
Dragonstar ~ William Oribello

The connection between humans and crystals is especially vivid in the following verses from the Vedas (Hindu sacred texts):

There is an endless net of threads
Throughout the universe.
The horizontal threads are in space.
The vertical threads are in time.
At every crossing of the threads,
There is an individual,
And every individual
Is a crystal bead.
The great light of absolute being
Illuminates and penetrates
Every crystal bead, and also,
Every crystal bead reflects
Not only the light
From every other crystal in the net,
But also every reflection
Of every reflection
Throughout the universe.

CHOOSING THE RIGHT MONEY DRAWING STONE

Ancient shaman's and priests believed that crystals and gemstones had a unique energy pattern and a place of origin in the physical universe. It was thought that each type of gemstone on Earth was a living entity and each had an important purpose and place in our lives.

Gemstones have often been given mystic qualities without a genuine understanding of the true nature of their potential. The early Egyptians and Atlanteans understood and explored the vast power and purposes within the crystal world. However, it has not been until recently that this information has been reexamined.

DIVINE MONEY SPELLS
Dragonstar ~ William Oribello

The knowledge and wisdom of the gemstone kingdom was very simple and direct. It has always been about self-empowerment. It was not what the stones could do for us, but that they were keys or portals to unlock our own potential and spiritual/psychic power.

Gemstones emit a loving, healing energy, and each has its own "personality." Each type of gemstone resonates with its own unique energy and vibration. A crystal or gemstone's character is determined by the different types minerals contained within. Their colors also dictate the spiritual and mystical nature that is different with each individual stone.

Our universe is one of vibrations. The regular motion of electrons in their orbits around an atom's nucleus produces vibrations that travel out through space and time. In some substances these vibrations tend to cancel one another due to the chaotic structure of that substance. But other substances, like crystals, have structures that allow these vibrations to add together. These vibrations are subtle, but they can be used to help you handle many of life's everyday problems.

Stones and crystals each have a unique structure and composition. This gives each one a unique vibration rate and quality. Your body is made of the same elements found in stones and crystals. Your body and its internal organs is a collection of parts, each with a specific structure (on a chemical level), and each made of different combinations of carbon, hydrogen, and other elements.

Since stones and crystals vibrate and emit pure, strong vibrations at constant rates, they can be used to help eliminate the distortions and restore proper balance, and can lead to better overall physical and mental well being. Each stone and crystal emits subtle vibrations that influence a specific area of your body. Matching the stone or crystal to its specific use allows you to get the most benefit from these natural gifts of harmony.

DIVINE MONEY SPELLS
Dragonstar ~ William Oribello

Crystals are the evolutionary peak of the mineral world. They represent perfection of structure, and are entities of a kind little understood by our modern world. Let them help you grow, love, heal, and be in harmony with the natural world around you.

There is a rich tradition stretching back for centuries for the magickal correspondences and purposes of crystals and gemstones. The Mystic Lodge of Dragonstar has a number of ancient books in its libraries detailing the purpose and uses for each crystal, gemstone and metal known to man.

Here is a list for some of the most popular stones currently available for people interested in Divine Money Spells. Even if you have no desire to use crystals and gemstones for magickal purposes, the simple act of carrying a certain stone with you will impart its unique vibration for your benefit.

Amazonite
Aventurine
Bloodstone
Calcite
Cat's-eye
Chrysoprase
Coal
Emerald
Jade
Marble
Mother-of-Pearl
Opal
Pearl
Peridot
Ruby
Salt

DIVINE MONEY SPELLS
Dragonstar ~ William Oribello

Sapphire
Tiger's-eye
Topaz
Green Tourmaline
Zircon

Let's not forget Quartz crystal, probably the most versatile crystal available for almost everyone. Quartz crystal can be programmed to do almost any kind of Divine Gemstone Magick. It aids psychic ability and when placed beneath the pillow it produces psychic dreams and ensures peaceful sleep. It is protective when worn and it amplifies any kind of Magick ritual.

Quartz is also used for purification, meditation, and channeling energy. Quartz helps balance the elements needed to make us whole and fulfilled and amplifies psychic energies.

PREPARING YOUR STONE FOR MAGICK

There are as many cleaning rituals and techniques as there are stones and crystals. Here are several techniques for the cleansing, purification, and charging of your crystals in preparation for Divine Money Spells.

There are a few words of caution that needs to be offered here. Some crystals are sensitive to water or light. Some become scratched easily. Some crystals are very sensitive and soluble in water. It is best not to use any soaking or immersion methods of cleaning with such crystals as Halite, Selenite, Lapis Lazuli, Malachite, Rhodizite, Turquoise, some Calcite and Celestite.

Others are very heat/light sensitive, so putting them out in the sunshine for an extended period of time may damage the color. Crystals that are heat/light sensitive are Amethyst, Rose Quartz, Turquoise, Malachite, Tourmaline, Fluorite, some Lapis

Lazuli and Quartz, which may fracture with sudden temperature changes.

A lot of the softer crystals are easily scratched since their composition is made up of softer materials. Such crystals are Celestite, Calcite, Malachite, Rhodochrosite, Fluorite, Selenite, Moonstone, Sodalite, Turquoise, Hematite, Apatite and Lapis Lazuli. Of course, if these happen to be tumbled, the likelihood of scratching is minimized.

The easiest way to cleanse your crystals is to put them under some type of running water (I prefer using fresh rain water myself) and as the water flows over your stones, visualize all the negativity and/or old energies flowing down the drain with the water. You can do each of stone individually, but they can all be done at once if time is tight.

This next technique comes from Scott Cunningham's book entitled *Crystal, Gem and Metal Magic*, Chapter 7, page 31 entitled "Cleansing the Stones."

"The simplest is to place the stones in full sunlight for a day, three days or even a week. The Sun's rays do the work here, burning away the unnecessary energies. Place the stones in direct sunlight. An inside window ledge isn't as good as an outdoor location because window glass blocks some of the Sun's rays. Remove the stones each day at dusk. Some stones will be 'clear' after a day's soaking up the rays. Others will need longer periods of time. Check the stones daily and sense the energies within them by placing them in your receptive hand. If the vibrations are regular, healthy, the cleansing has been successful."

NOTE: Caution should be taken when using sunlight to clear your stones. Many stones color tends to fade in the sun. Also internal fractures may cause your stone to crack or break if placed in the sun.

DIVINE MONEY SPELLS
Dragonstar ~ William Oribello

Another technique is to soak the crystal in brown rice for twenty-four hours. The rice balances and centers the energy, removing the negativity, while dissipating and transforming the negative to the positive. Upon completion of the 'soak' the rice is purified and energized and is excellent and nutritious to eat.

You can also soak the crystal in flowers [e.g., rose petals, orange blossoms, honeysuckle, etc.] for twenty four hours; the essence strips away negativity and cleanses the stone while the purity and energy of the flower is transmitted to the stone.

Moonlight is another way of clearing your gemstones. Simply place outside from the Full to the New Moon. Waning moons are good times to clear crystals, to dispel old energies, but any time works. The amount of time used varies with the sensitivity of the healer and the amount of material from which the stone needs cleansing. Try hanging your gemstone necklaces in a tree where the moonlight can cleanse them.

It is recommended that you cleanse new crystals and gemstones before you begin working with them, as well as when you have finished a Divine Money Spell. Crystals absorb ambient vibrations from their surroundings and the people they come into contact with. Crystals generously donate their energy to foster healing, love and light. Drained crystals are particularly vulnerable to stress when exposed to dense energy or a toxic environment.

DEDICATING AND PROGRAMMING YOUR CRYSTALS

After you have cleared your gemstone or crystal, it is a good idea to dedicate it or program it. The purpose of programming a crystal or gemstone is to focus its abilities on something you specifically need, thereby magnifying the stone's intent through your own.

Dedicating your crystal is a simple process that requires only a few quiet moments and defines your intention for co-creation. Your intention, during the dedication, describes to your crystal how you want it to work with you and sets the crystal's light vibration in harmony with your intentions.

Visualize the idea of "love, light and for the good of all" as part of your activation. Doing so will neutralize any subconscious vibrations that could influence this process. Focus on the positive as you bond with your crystal. For example, "I affirm abundance and prosperity for myself and all beings." Or, "I am ever protected by the Light. Good comes to me and good comes from me."

For Divine Money Spells, begin your dedication ceremony with your intentions identified clearly to yourself. Ask the Universe to bless the mission for which you are dedicating your crystal.

The purpose of dedicating the stone to a high level healing energy or Goddess (God) Creator is to protect it from negative energy. A crystal or stone that is programmed and dedicated in these ways becomes much more powerful and useful as a tool.

This is a very simple process. Hold the crystal or gemstone in your hand and sense its energy. With the stone being newly cleared, the energy will feel stronger and even more appealing that before. As you sense this energy and appreciate it, ask quietly to be connected to the deva of the crystal or gemstone. Though not animate, stones are living things and the deva of the piece is the stone's life-force energy.

Once you feel you have sensed what you can from the energy, think of what you will be using the stone for. Think of these uses, and then quietly ask the gemstone if it is willing to act in the way you wish. The crystals energy may increase with a yes or seem to disappear with a no. If the stone accepts your intent, state in your mind that it be so.

Once a stone is programmed, it will hold its intent until you or someone else reprograms it. To prevent any negative energy from attaching itself to your crystal you may with to dedicate it. To do this, simply hold the crystal or gemstone in your hand and state clearly in your mind:

"Only the most positive high-level energy may work through this healing tool."

Focus on your intent for a while, and then end your sensing (meditation) with "SO BE IT." The stone is now dedicated.

After dedicating your crystal or gemstone you can now program it for a specific task. Formulate a precise phrase which accurately describes the nature of the programming. i.e., money, success, prosperity, free of debts, etc.

Hold the crystal in the left hand (if left-handed, hold the crystal in the right hand), relax for several minutes, initiate circular breathing, and center the consciousness. Consciously align the personal conscious awareness with the higher self and/or other predefined appropriate otherworldly beings.

Ask for guidance, protection, and assistance in the programming process. Open the center of consciousness and allow receptivity to flow through the inner being. Repeat the formulated phrase 20-30 times in succession while visualizing and/or feeling the desired effect of the program. As the phrase is repeated, an energy field will build and culminate in the energy pattern necessary to represent the desired program.

While maintaining full awareness of the energy field, bring total awareness and consciousness to the area of the third-eye or heart chakra. Place the crystal in front of the area of the third-eye or heart chakra and allow the self to feel the connection with it.

Direct the energy field into the crystal for 30-60 seconds and allow the program to be transferred to within the crystal. Intuitive recognition will signal when the transmittal is complete. Detach consciousness from the crystal and allow the universal energies to act.

Any crystal or gemstone can be programmed by projecting and holding a thought during meditation. For example, if you are experiencing anxiety about debt, hold the point of a clear, quartz crystal up to your forehead and visualize yourself as being calm, secure, confident, and having money spontaneously flowing to solve the situation.

Project this thought form into the crystal and then sit quietly, holding the crystal as you mentally reaffirm to yourself the positive reality you have created. This crystal can them be carried with you, to be held, looked at, or thought of during the prepared event. The crystal retains the programmed thought and will emanate that vision back to you.

It is possible to program your crystal or other stone to hold a message, work for a specific purpose, broadcast an affirmation or emotion, enhance protective filters, communication, meditation, healing work and an almost infinite number of other purposes. Before there were computers, this was called "enchanting."

It is quite important when programming a crystal by intention that you are clear and focused on just what it is that you intend to do. Some crystals will come to you with a strong vibration for a specific purpose. It is not appropriate to use this kind of stone for purposes other than what it was naturally intended to do. Use your intuitive sense and listen to what a stone is saying before you start any programming session.

TAROT MONEY SPELL

Try this excellent Divine Money Spell to get the cash flowing in your direction. You need a green candle, your favorite money-drawing oil and one small piece of aventurine.

DIVINE MONEY SPELLS

Dragonstar ~ William Oribello

On the night of a new moon, anoint a green candle with money-drawing oil (virgin olive-oil will work as well), rubbing towards yourself from wick to base since you are trying to attract something to you.

Take the Ace of Pentacles card from the Tarot deck and place it face up behind the candle. The Ace of Pentacles represents money coming to you, wealth and general success. Sit and gaze at the Ace of Pentacles card as it glows with the light of the candle flame. Think about money coming to you. Think about ways you can get it.

Try to actually see the money in your possession and think about what you will do with it when it is yours. Leave the card and candle in position for a good long while, visualizing money coming to you from seen and unseen sources.

Then with supreme concentration, blow the candle out and rub your hands together in the smoke imagining that you are rubbing money between your hands. Leave the extinguished candle and the Ace of Pentacles in place. The next night, anoint the candle and light it again. Draw the Six of Pentacles and place it counterclockwise to the Ace.

Visualize yourself as wealthy enough to spread the money around, to your friends, family and to those in need. When the time is right, blow out the candle, rubbing your hands in the smoke, leave the extinguished candle and cards in place. On the following night, repeat the anointing (if by this time you require a new candle because the old one has burnt down, that is no problem, just make sure it is a green one) and light the candle.

Draw the Page of Pentacles and place it to the left of the six. Visualize yourself receiving news of money coming to you from expected and unexpected sources. Meditate on this and with full concentration, blow the candle out and rub your hands in the smoke. Leave cards and candle in place.

DIVINE MONEY SPELLS
Dragonstar ~ William Oribello

The following night, perform the same sequence, this time placing the Ten of Pentacles to the left of the Page. The Ten represents the culmination of wealth and material security. Envision being in this position of security. As before, blow out the candle and rub your hands in the smoke.

On the final night of the working, light the candle and place either the Queen of Pentacles (if you are female) or the King of Pentacles (if you are male) at the top of the spread. Know you have the power to move money and prosperity into your life. Meditate on this power you have to shape your own destiny. Now say out loud in a commanding voice:

Money and good fortune come to me.
The Universe provides me with opportunities and sources of wealth.
As I cast this spell, I send its' power out into the universe to do my bidding!

Now blow out the candle, rub your hands in the smoke and say:

Just as my hands are full of this smoke, so will they be full of money.

Place the aventurine on top of the cards and leave the spread in place until the morning after the night of the full moon and then return the cards to the Tarot pack. This powerful spell only needs to be preformed once for it to work.

DIVINE MONEY SPELLS
Dragonstar ~ William Oribello

NEW YEAR'S STONE

Here is a simple spell for money and prosperity using an ordinary stone. At sunrise on the morning of the New Year, light one green candle and place it on a table in the house. Go outside and find the largest stone you can carry. Take this back to your house and put it in a place of prominence. Allow the candle to burn completely out. If you keep the stone in your house for a year, it will be one filled with money, success and prosperity. Replace the stone with a new one every new year.

MAGICK MONEY BOX

For this money spell you will need: One small box, one green candle, one small calcite gemstone or polished gemstone that is green in color, patchouli oil, cedar shavings, nutmeg powder, two cinnamon sticks, two quarters, two dimes, two nickels, two pennies, paper and green pencil or marker.

Rub the candle with the oil, empower it with your energy and light it. Draw your need on the paper (draw an unpaid bill that's worrying you, or groceries-whatever you need money for). Always draw with power and visualize your need.

Charge each ingredient with the command to draw money to you, then place on the paper while visualizing. Next, pick up the paper and scoop the ingredients into the box, light the paper in the candle flame and place it in an ashtray or other fireproof container to burn while visualizing your need being fulfilled. Snuff the candle out when you are finished.

Now take the money out of the box and put it in your pocket or purse. Take the box and hide it under your bed and relight the candle every night for 13 minutes while visualizing money coming your way. Do this until the candle is gone. Remove the box, throw away the contents except for the calcite – the stone can be recharged and used again. Your spell should work by the time the candle has melted away.

GEMSTONE AND STRING SPELL

You will need three green candles, one small quartz crystal and a length of string seven inches in length for this old-fashioned, yet powerful spell. First, write down the reason you need money and fold the paper once. Next, arrange the candles into a triangle with the paper in the middle and the crystal placed directly on top.

Take the length of string and start to tie knots along its length. With each knot, say one of the lines to this spell.

By knot of one, my spell's begun
By knot of two, plenty fruitful work to do
By knot of three, money comes to me
By knot of four, opportunity knocks at my door
By knot of five, my business thrives
By knot of six, this spell is fixed
By knot of seven, success in given
By knot of eight, increase is great
By knot of nine, these things are mine!

After saying this spell, take the paper with your desire written on it and light it with one of the candles. Place the paper in an ashtray or fireproof container to burn out. It is now safe to snuff out the candles.

Wrap the knotted string around the crystal so it binds tightly against the stone. Place the crystal and string in a safe place for one month. Your desire should appear before the end of the month. Afterwards, take the string off the crystal and recharge the stone for later use.

MONEY SPELL BY THE LIGHT OF THE FULL MOON

Here is an old Celtic spell using one small white candle and one green-colored stone of your choice. Fill a clear glass with fresh rain water and drop your gemstone and a silver coin into it. Position the glass so that the light from the moon shines into the water. Gently sweep your hands just above the surface, symbolically gathering the moon's silver. While doing this say the following chant:

> *Lovely Lady of the Moon, bring to me your wealth right soon. Fill my hands with silver and gold. All you give, my purse can hold.*

Repeat this three times. When finished, pour the water upon the earth and visualize money and success growing out of the ground like grain in a summer's field. Take the green gemstone and store it in a safe, dark place until the next full moon. If this spell does not work in the first month, repeat once more with the same stone, but a fresh silver coin. The stone can be saved and recharged for future use.

DIVINE MONEY SPELLS

Dragonstar ~ William Oribello

THE NINE DAY MONEY SPELL

This spell can be done at any time, but preferably at the same time each day or night. You will need a green candle and a white candle. The green candle represents the money, and the white candle represents you. You will also need one green tourmaline, or a quartz crystal that you have charge with money vibrations. Make sure you anoint the candles with oil first, thinking of your desire for money to come to you. Set the candles on a table nine inches apart with your gemstone placed between them. After doing this say out loud:

Money, money come to me
In abundance three times three
May I be enriched in the best of ways
Harming none on its way
This I accept, so it be
Bring me money three times three!

Repeat this spell for nine days. Each day move the white candle one inch closer to the green candle. When the candles touch the crystal, your spell is finished. Make sure you visualize the money pouring in from the universe. The crystal can now be recharged for future use.

SAGE AND GEMSTONE WEALTH SPELL

For wealth and prosperity for a year, take the husk from an ear of corn and put a dollar bill, along with a piece of coal and this message written on a fresh piece of white paper:

Oh, dear god of luck
money is like muck

not good except it be spread
Spread some here at _____
(write in your address).
Thanks be to thee. Amen!

Sign your name and Sprinkle the dollar bill, gemstone and note with sage. Roll the husk up and tie together with green string or ribbon. Dangle the token over a burning, white candle so it is infused with smoke. Hang the token up above the entryway of your house with green cord.

That husk should bring riches into your home or business by the bushel. Repeat the spell once a year at the same time each year with fresh ingredients. The gemstone can be recharged and used for another spell, but not the same money spell. Take the old dollar bill and give it to the poor or a charity.

ROSE QUARTZ MONEY SPELL

To inspire others to give you money, place your gemstone in a small saucer and moisten it with fresh rain water. Get a ball of green cord or yarn and wind it around your crystal, winding until the stone is completely covered and secure. Tie the cord so that the ball will not unwind and hang above the doorway. All those who enter will become possessed with an unreasoning desire to bring gifts and money to your home. Place the wrapped crystal in a window once a month during the full moon to preserve it's powers.

DIVINE MONEY SPELLS
Dragonstar ~ William Oribello

MAGNETIC MONEY SPELL

To find money, one should make a conjure bag containing a lodestone or a regular magnet to attract and draw wealth to you. Include in the bag some smartweed to enable you to see how to capture wealth and hold it without being led astray by unprofitable distractions or foolish delays. Feed your money bag with a sprinkle of money-drawing incense every third day until you find the amount you need.

THREE GEMSTONE MONEY SPELL

A lucky gemstone money spell is made by taking three stones of your choice and placing them in a bag. The gemstones should be charged to attract money and prosperity. A good choice would be two pieces of quartz and any stone that is green in color.

Now take seven different types of money, such as a penny, nickel, dime, quarter, a half dollar, $1.00 bill, and $5.00 bill, all of which are sprinkled liberally with lavender.

Take the bag with you for seven days and your money should multiply seven times (this would give you $41.46 above your original investment) or, in some instances if the fates are smiling in your direction, seven times seven. This would result in a tidy sum of $338.50 and seems well worth to give this spell a try.

After one month, take all ingredients out of the bag and cleanse them by placing them around a burning white candle. When the candle has completely burned out, place them back into the bag for another month.

DIVINE MONEY SPELLS
Dragonstar ~ William Oribello

A QUICK MONEY SPELL

This spell is intended to attract money to pay off an unexpected bill or debt. Take a green candle and anoint it with cinnamon oil. Place at the foot of the candle one moonstone that has been charged by the new moon to attract money. Take the bill or write on a piece of clean, white paper the amount of a bill you owe and who it is to. Place the paper under the candle. Now, pick up the moonstone and clasping it tightly in your hands over the candle and say out loud in a commanding voice:

This candle burns to light the way
for the money I need to pay this bill
in a way that harms no one!

Light the candle and burn patchouli incense. Meditate for about five minutes as the candle burns. Visualize you writing the check or purchasing the money order for this bill and putting it in the mail. You can now snuff the candle out. Burn the candle every day around the same time for seven days and 15 minutes at a time. Also, burn patchouli incense every day along with the candle. On the last day, burn the paper with the flame from the candle and let the candle burn completely out.

GEMSTONE DOLL PROSPERITY SPELL

You will first need to make a doll out of green cloth. You don't have to be an artist to do this. A crude image with arms and legs will do just fine, just make sure you leave the head open to apply the special ingredients. You will also need one white candle, chamomile for money, rosemary for luck and basil for success.

DIVINE MONEY SPELLS

Dragonstar ~ William Oribello

Now pick a crystal or gemstone of any type and charge it to draw prosperity to you. Some people will pick a green colored stone to represent money, but you can use any type of crystal or gemstone that feels right to you.

Light the white candle and place it in the middle of a small table in the center of a room. Lay out your ingredients on the table and one by one, place a pinch of each herb into the open head of you doll, leaving the gemstone until last.

As you place each item into the doll, say out loud:

With these herbs and stone
money and prosperity come to me
with harm to none!

Now seal the head up with a needle and thread, or tape. Place your money doll at the foot of the candle and walk three times around the table. As you walk around the table, imagine a green, soothing mist trailing from your fingers, enveloping you and enclosing your Magick circle. With each circle, repeat the following:

I conjure the magick circle
I am safe within the Goddess' womb
A sacred place, a world apart
Where enchantment births and magick starts
With Air and Fire, Water and Earth
I circle round the Mother's girth this circle is sealed!

When you are finished with your spell, allow the candle to burn out on its own. Take your money doll and place it under your bed for one month. Your spell should take effect within one month of casting.

DIVINE MONEY SPELLS
Dragonstar ~ William Oribello

GEMSTONE HAIR MONEY SPELL

There are times when we are sometimes faced with an urgent financial need. This is one spell to use only when you are in a real financial bind. Do not misuse the powers for greediness, only to help you out in a pinch if the need arises.

This may not work well for those of you with short hair or no hair. If this is the case, try substituting green thread/yarn (use natural fiber such as cotton/wool). To see if the yarn is real wool or synthetic, burn a bit of it on the end. If it forms a hard little nub, then it is synthetic.

Brush/comb your hair. The strands of hair that are on your comb/brush, is what you'll be using. When you have at least nine or more long strands of hair, you are ready to begin. Place the strands of hair in front of you and hold them down with a money-drawing crystal or gemstone of your choice. Pick a stone that seems to radiate money and wealth. If in doubt, take a smoky quartz crystal and charge it with money-drawing energies. Allow the stone to sit on the strands of hair for seven minutes. Now begin chanting the following or similar words:

Dear Lord and Lady
Please send money to me
Please send money to me
Dear Lord and Lady
Let the money come in an innocent way
Let harm come to none for fulfilling
this need for which I pray!

As you chant the, rub the stands of hair between your palms, to form a sort of cord. Keep chanting, while doing the following. Next, tie nine knots onto this hair cord in the following order – the numbers represent where the knots should be tied.

-1—6—4—8—3—7—5—9—2-

DIVINE MONEY SPELLS
Dragonstar ~ William Oribello

Tie the first knot at the furthest left side of the hair cord, the second knot at the furthest right side of the hair cord, the third knot in the middle and so on. As you tie these knots, keep chanting. Visualize your financial need being met, through positive ways, such as finding a stash of money you forgot about, winning a small sum, but not through inheritances etc. (as this is destructive, you don't want someone to die in order for you to meet your financial needs. That is why the wording of the chant used is so important).

Once you have tied the nine knots in the appropriate order, keep chanting and visualizing debts paid in full etc. Then, tie the hair cord around your money-drawing crystal and place it in a small box or bag. Place the box or bag in a dark corner of a closet or under your bed. When your money problems have ended, take everything apart and either bury the hair cord, burn it, or throw it into the wind and recharge the crystal for future use.

It has been recommended to then make an offering to the Lord and Lady by either burying an apple, pour some milk/wine/beer into the ground, bury a bit of tobacco etc. As you prepare and leave your offering of thanks, say out loud that you are thankful for their love, assistance, help, guidance and be sincere when doing so.

RUMANIAN CRYSTAL MONEY SPELL

Place a small bowl or cup in a place you will see it every day. Hold in your dominant hand three coins of any denomination and three small gemstones that have been cleansed and charged to draw money. Now say out loud in a commanding voice:

DIVINE MONEY SPELLS

Dragonstar ~ William Oribello

Trinka five, Trinka five
Ancient spirits come alive
Money grow and money thrive
Spirits of the Trinka Five

Toss the coins and stones in the container. Repeat the spell daily, tossing the three coins and three stones in the dish each day for nine consecutive days. Then continue doing the spell once a week until you have the money you need.

MONEY GEMSTONE

Find a gemstone that's nearly square in shape. Anoint a green candle with oil and place in a holder and light. Now, by the glow of the candle, paint or draw a dollar sign onto the stone with gold paint or ink (gold glitter glue works as well).

As you paint or draw, visualize the stone drawing money into your life. See yourself enjoying the money for whatever purpose it will be used for. Let the stone sit in the light from the candle for seven minutes. Snuff out the candles flame. Let the candle burn for seven minutes a day until gone and keep the stone with you as a talisman for drawing money and good fortune to you.

93

DIVINE MONEY SPELLS
Dragonstar ~ William Oribello

CLEANSE AND BRING CUSTOMERS, MONEY, SUCCESS TO A BUSINESS

When opening a new business as in moving into a new residence, it is always wise (and in some cultures, customary) to clear away any negative vibes remaining from past tenants or merchants by either washing down the premises (cleaning walls and floor etc.) with a spiritual cleaning mixture such as Van Van oil in a bit of hot soapy water or some Rue water.

Some other good choices for clearing away old influences are to use a White Sage smudge stick to cleanse the area or to burn cleansing and purifying incense such as Dragons Blood, benzoin, mesquite wood or Copal as you recite the 23rd Psalm. One can also burn traditional Sahumerio incense on charcoal (usually contains such things as garlic skins, cinnamon, anise, eucalyptus, rosemary etc.).

After the cleansing, try such things as these to draw customers to your place of business and increase your chances of prosperity and success. Place a mixture of sassafras and bayberry bark in your cash drawer and or light a white candle anointed with bayberry and sassafras oil and let it burn in your place of business.

Burn an incense blend of benzoin, copal and cinnamon to bring about better business or Allspice mixed with Gloria incense to bring about success, wealth and prosperity.

Put earthsmoke in your shoes or make into a tea and use it as sprinkling water outside you business for success and quick money gains.

Place four quartz crystals in four corners of your main room and keep them there for one month. After one month, cleanse the stones and recharge them for future use.

94

DIVINE MONEY SPELLS
Dragonstar ~ William Oribello

CRYSTAL MONEY DOUBLING SPELL

This spells helps double any denomination of cash paper money that you have. First find some almost new cash paper money in the largest denomination possible. A twenty or fifty dollar bill is good. You will also need a good money gemstone for this spell.

Calcite is a good choice, not only because of its money-drawing characteristics, but calcite is also good for doubling the strength of spells. Used in combination with a money or prosperity spell, calcite will greatly enhance your chances of a successful spell.

Place this in a white envelope along with a small piece of calcite, seal and fold the envelope. Light three green candles and place them to form a triangle. With the envelope in the center of the triangle say out loud in a commanding voice:

Universal powers to me shall bring
The way to double this sum
Hear me, thou spirits which sing
Swiftly and quietly come!

Hold the envelope up, and pretend that it has become heavier. Snuff the candles out and repeat this once every day for seven days. Keep the envelope in your bedroom.

After you receive more money, open the envelope and either spend, or deposit the money that was in the envelope. The calcite can be cleansed and recharged for future use.

DIVINE MONEY SPELLS
Dragonstar ~ William Oribello

LUCKY MONEY

Cast the ultimate good luck spell to draw money and prosperity to you. You will need two quartz crystals that you have personally charged to attract money and wealth. You also will need some play paper money – the larger the denominations, the better. Two green candles and one white, large enough to last nine days, nine minutes a day. Nine cloves, one whole nutmeg, lucky Oil – made from equal parts of pure virgin olive oil and rose oil, (rose oil is available at any store that sells essential oils), and finally a $1.00, $5.00, or $10.00 bill that you won't mind donating later.

Inscribe your name down the front of the white candle, using a twig from a green tree. On each green candle inscribe three dollar signs. Dip your finger in the Lucky Oil and rub it all over the candles, repeating nine times:

By the power of the elements, I empower you!

Set the candles on a table where they will not be disturbed, except by you for nine days. Put the white candle between the two green candles and a crystal at either end.

Surround the candles completely with the play money, reserving two large denomination bills. Sprinkle the cloves on top of the money. Wrap the whole nutmeg up in your real money. Place it in front of the candle with your name on it.

Each day for nine days burn the candle for nine minutes. During these nine minutes you should concentrate on your luck with money; how you will make the right decisions concerning money, how money will come to you through lotteries, gambling, and any lucky money.

On the ninth day, let the candles burn out completely while you concentrate on your petition. On the ninth day, take the real money unwrapped from the nutmeg and give it to what you consider a good cause.

DIVINE MONEY SPELLS
Dragonstar ~ William Oribello

On the ninth day, put all the equipment used in the spell together in a safe place. At the end of nine days you may discard the equipment discreetly keeping it all together. Burial is the preferred form of discarding.

NOTE: Keep the nutmeg in your purse, pocket, or wallet as a good luck charm. Use the cloves in cooking when you want to feel especially lucky. The crystals can be cleansed, recharged and used again in the future.

FLOWING MONEY

For this spell you will need a bowl, four pinches of green tea, four pinches of rosemary, one Aventurine gemstone. Mix all the ingredients in the bowl. Mix them together by using the fingers of your power hand (your right hand if you are right handed, and vice versa). Place the stone into the mix. As you mix them, chant:

Currency come to me and grow,
Money come to me and flow.
So be it! Make it so!

Now empty the bowl with the stone into a small bag of cotton, special or wool. Take this bag to a place where there is flowing water (such as a brook, or the ocean, a stream, etc.) and empty the bag's contents into the water.

DIVINE MONEY SPELLS
Dragonstar ~ William Oribello

DIVINE MONEY SPELLS
Dragonstar ~ William Oribello

CHAPTER FIVE – MONEY SPELLS FROM THE HOLY SCRIPTURE

The idea behind Magick from the Holy Scripture is simple; all verses in the Bible are charged with spiritual energies. This power of creation is called "LOGOS," meaning "WORD." It is thought that God the Creator used the LOGOS to initiate creation. The Universe and everything within it are divine words that have solidified. You can imagine that they were once dissolved in the sound vibrations of the divine cosmic word. Each thing we see is a divine word become solid.

In this way we can understand the deeper meaning of the beginning of *The Gospel According to John*:

'In the beginning was the Word,
and the Word was with God,
and a God was the Word.

The Word was with God at the beginning,
and through it all things came to be;
no single thing was created without it.'

Everything that came into existence emerged from the Word.

For centuries, people have been using the Holy Scripture to induce magickal principles. Some of this has come down to us in the magickal practices of Hoodoo and Folk Magick.

The majority of these ancient techniques have been handed down from generation to generation strictly by word of mouth and little has actually ever been written down. Because of this, the secret of Holy Scripture Magick has been kept within small groups scattered across the globe. Many have no idea that other practitioners of the ancient art even exist. The rise of evangelical Christianity has forced many adepts to go underground, or even give up practicing altogether.

For a long time churches have taught that all Magick is inherently evil and that anyone who practices it is to be condemned and possibly even put to death. This has little actually to do with a few verses in the Bible that speak against witches and diviners, and more to do with the churches power base that has held control over the people for centuries.

It is our divine right as children of Creation to understand and glorify the secrets of the Universe. God, the Creative force of reality has provided for us the powers of creation, handed down from the Eons in the form of words that resonate with the energies of Creation. Despite what the ministers, priests and imams have tried to suppress, the power of Creation is within all of us, and it is Gods will that we use these powers to comprehend and eventually rejoice with Him the ultimate beauty of Creation.

As with any kind of Magick, you first have to get yourself in the right state of mind. You want to have a quiet, private location to work your spell. It is imperative that you can spend at least a half an hour by yourself without any interruptions.

You next want to clearly envision what your spell is going to accomplish. This is extremely important, for unless you have a clear goal in mind, your spell will be useless. This is what ultimately dooms most spells to failure - the inability to clearly and concisely envision what your need is. The human mind has an unpleasant habit of not being able to hold its attention on any one subject for more than a few seconds at a time. Our thoughts tend to constantly jump around from one issue to another, never allowing our consciousness to focus on one idea or desire for any length of time. This is why learning how to meditate is an excellent practice for anyone wishing to learn to practice Divine Money Spells.

DIVINE MONEY SPELLS
Dragonstar ~ William Oribello

So take some time to meditate on what it is you wish to accomplish with your Magick spell. Another good method is to write down what you want to happen with your spell.

Take a plain piece of white paper and write down your desire or need. Keep it simple, and state clearly what it is you want to happen.

For example, if you are looking for a new job, write down: "I will soon find a new and better job."

Don't write: "I wish I could find a new and better job."

You have to make a statement on what you want to happen. Not a wish. You are telling the universe that you WILL find a new job.

The same goes for a money and prosperity spell. Write down: "I will receive money and prosperity with harm to no one."

Once again, don't put down: "I wish I will receive money and prosperity with harm to no one." You have to use your powers of creation to make your desire happen by focusing on what WILL happen. Not by focusing on wishing something to happen.

Also, don't hope for something to happen. Don't write down, or concentrate on "hoping" something will happen. You have to COMMAND it to happen.

God the Creator did not say: "I hope there will be light." He said: "Let there be light!" And it was so. Since you are a part of creation, you have also been given the powers of Creation. When you cast your spell, you are using your abilities to CREATE your desires. So don't play around, state clearly and with confidence what you want.

"I WILL get a new and better job!" "I WILL make more money!" "I WILL have good luck!"

DIVINE MONEY SPELLS
Dragonstar ~ William Oribello

Find out what you want in your life, and then make it happen!

USING THE BIBLE TO RECEIVE NEEDED MONEY

We all have times when money is a little tight, so let's do a Bible Verse spell to bring in a small amount of money. Concentrate, or write down what you want to occur: "I WILL get enough money to tide me over."

You may also want to add a stipulation that this money is only to come to you without harming anyone else in the process. After all, money does not grow on trees, it has to come from somewhere, and you don't want to take something that doesn't rightfully belong to you and belongs to someone else

Focus on your desire for a little extra money. Now, repeat out loud the following Bible verse three times and repeat for three days at the same time each day:

Charge them that are rich in this world, that they be not highminded, nor trust in uncertain riches, but in the living God, who giveth us richly all things to enjoy; That they do good, that they be rich in good works, ready to distribute, willing to communicate; Laying up in store for themselves a good foundation against the time to come, that they may lay hold on eternal life.

(1 Timothy 6:17-19)

Money will arrive within three weeks.

DIVINE MONEY SPELLS
Dragonstar ~ William Oribello

GOOD FORTUNE IN BUSINESS AND MONEY

God is not man, that he should lie,
or a son of man, that he should change his mind.
Has he said, and will he not do it?
Or has he spoken, and will he not fulfill it?

Numbers 23:19

TO GET A BETTER JOB

For the Lamb which is in the midst of the throne shall feed them, and shall lead them unto living fountains of waters: and God shall wipe away all tears from their eyes.

Revelation 7:17

FOR SUCCESS IN BUSINESS

They shall be abundantly satisfied with the fatness of thy house; and thou shalt make them drink of the river of thy pleasures.

Psalms 36:8

DIVINE MONEY SPELLS
Dragonstar ~ William Oribello

RID YOURSELF OF TROUBLES WITH MONEY OR BUSINESS

I will also make it a possession for the bittern, and pools of water: and I will sweep it with the besom of destruction, saith the LORD of hosts.

Isaiah 14:23

RISE ABOVE ANY COMPETITION

A wise king scattereth the wicked, and bringeth the wheel over them.

Proverbs 20:26

SUCCESS FROM UNFAIR COMPETITION

The wrath of God came upon them, and slew the fattest of them, and smote down the chosen men of Israel.

Psalms 78:31

DIVINE MONEY SPELLS
Dragonstar ~ William Oribello

TO ATTRACT CUSTOMERS

And the multitudes gave heed with one accord unto the things that were spoken by Philip, when they heard, and saw the signs which he did.

Acts 8:6

CONTACT YOUR GUARDIAN ANGEL TO HELP WITH MONEY PROBLEMS

They are of the world: therefore speak they of the world, and the world heareth them.

1 John 4:5

GOOD LUCK WITH MONEY

Sing unto Jehovah a new song, and his praise from the end of the earth; ye that go down to the sea, and all that is therein, the isles, and the inhabitants thereof.

Isaiah 42:10

DIVINE MONEY SPELLS
Dragonstar ~ William Oribello

SEVEN DAYS OF GOOD LUCK WITH MONEY

Yea, thou doest away with fear, And hinderest devotion before God.

Job 15:4

CHANGE YOUR LUCK WITH MONEY AND DEPTS

And on my behalf, that utterance may be given unto me in opening my mouth, to make known with boldness the mystery of the gospel.

Ephesians 6:19

FIND LOST MONEY OR VALUABLES

For he bringeth down them that dwell on high; the lofty city, he layeth it low; he layeth it low, even to the ground; he bringeth it even to the dust.

Isaiah 26:5

DIVINE MONEY SPELLS

Dragonstar ~ William Oribello

SUCCESS IN THE LOTTERY

And take double money in your hand; and the money that was brought again in the mouth of your sacks, carry it again in your hand; peradventure it was an oversight:

Genesis 43:12

SUCCESS WITHOUT HURTING OTHERS

He that hath knowledge spareth his words: and a man of understanding is of an excellent spirit.

Proverbs 17:27

SPELL FOR WEALTH AND PROSPERITY

Bring ye all the tithes into the storehouse, that there may be meat in mine house, and prove me now herewith, saith the Lord of hosts, if I will not open you the windows of heaven, and pour you out a blessing, that there shall not be room enough to receive it.

Malachi 3:10

DIVINE MONEY SPELLS
Dragonstar ~ William Oribello

BANISH DEBT FOREVER

He that receiveth a prophet in the name of a prophet shall receive a prophet's reward: and he that receiveth a righteous man in the name of a righteous man shall receive a righteous man's reward.

Matthew 10:41

BE MORE RESPONSIBLE WITH MONEY

The Lord of hosts hath sworn, saying, Surely as I have thought, so shall it come to pass; and as I have purposed, so shall it stand:

Isaiah 14:24

SPELL TO LOOK BEYOND MATERIAL POSSESSIONS

Lay not up for yourselves treasures upon the earth, where moth and rust consume, and where thieves break through and steal:

Matthew 6:19

DIVINE MONEY SPELLS
Dragonstar ~ William Oribello

SPELL TO HELP A FRIEND WHO HAS MONEY TROUBLES

The Lord hear thee in the day of trouble; the name of the God of Jacob defend thee;

Psalms 20:1

SPELL TO PROTECT YOUR HOME FROM FORCLOSURE

For I am persuaded that neither death nor life, nor angels nor principalities nor powers, nor things present nor things to come, nor height nor depth, nor any other created thing, shall be able to separate us from the love of God which is in Christ Jesus our Lord.

Romans 8:38-39

SPELL TO STOP THIEVES

Rob not the poor, because he is poor; Neither oppress the afflicted in the gate: For Jehovah will plead their cause, And despoil of life those that despoil them.

Proverbs 22:22

DIVINE MONEY SPELLS
Dragonstar ~ William Oribello

SPELL TO KNOW THE TRUTH ABOUT MONEY PROBLEMS

And if thou sell aught unto thy neighbor, or buy of thy neighbor's hand, ye shall not wrong one another.

Leviticus 25:14

SPELL TO INCREASE PSYCHIC POWERS TO FIND MONEY

For if the word spoken through angels proved stedfast, and every transgression and disobedience received a just recompense of reward; how shall we escape, if we neglect so great a salvation? which having at the first been spoken through the Lord, was confirmed unto us by them that heard; God also bearing witness with them, both by signs and wonders, and by manifold powers, and by gifts of the Holy Spirit, according to his own will.

Hebrews 2:2-4

SPELL TO ATTRACT WEALTH

Ask me, and I will give you the nations as your inheritance and the ends of the earth as your own possession.

Psalms 2:8

DIVINE MONEY SPELLS
Dragonstar ~ William Oribello

SPELL TO OBTAIN FINANCIAL FAVORS FROM IMPORTANT PEOPLE

I communed with mine own hear, saying, Lo, I have gotten me great wisdom above all that were before me in Jerusalem; yea, my heart hath had great experience of wisdom and knowledge.

Ecclesiastes 1:16

SPELL TO FIND INNER STRENGTH IN TIMES OF FINANCIAL CRISIS

Fear ye not me? saith Jehovah: will ye not tremble at my presence, who have placed the sand for the bound of the sea, by a perpetual decree, that it cannot pass it? and though the waves thereof toss themselves, yet can they not prevail; though they roar.

Jeremiah 5:22

SPELL TO TURN BAD LUCK INTO GOOD

And said, naked came I out of my mother's womb, and naked shall I return thither: the Lord gave, and the Lord hath taken away; blessed be the name of the Lord

Job 1:21

111

DIVINE MONEY SPELLS
Dragonstar ~ William Oribello

SPELL FOR SUCCESS IN MAKING MONEY

Bring ye all the tithes into the storehouse, that there may be meat in mine house, and prove me now herewith, saith the Lord of hosts, if I will not open you the windows of heaven, and pour you out a blessing, that there shall not be room enough to receive it.

Malachi 3:10

SPELL TO RECEIVE INSTRUCTIONS IN DREAMS ON HOW TO OVERCOME MONEY TROUBLES

Surely then shalt thou lift up thy face without spot; Yea, thou shalt be stedfast, and shalt not fear: For thou shalt forget thy misery; Thou shalt remember it as waters that are passed away, And `thy' life shall be clearer than the noonday; Though there be darkness, it shall be as the morning.

Job 11:15-17

SPELL FOR LUCK WITH THE LOTTERY

Honor the Lord with your possessions and with the first fruits of all your increase; so your barns will be filled with plenty, and your vats will overflow with new wine.

Proverbs 3:9-10

DIVINE MONEY SPELLS
Dragonstar ~ William Oribello

SPELL SO THAT DEBTS WILL BE REPAYED

Do not rob the poor because he is poor, nor oppress the afflicted at the gate; for the Lord will plead their cause, and plunder the soul of those who plunder them.

Proverbs 22:22-23

SPELL TO GET A DESERVED RAISE

Servants, in all things do the orders of your natural masters; not only when their eyes are on you, as pleasers of men, but with all your heart, fearing the Lord: Whatever you do, do it readily, as to the Lord and not to men.

Colossians 3:22-23

SPELL TO FIND LOST MONEY

Go, and cry in the ears of Jerusalem, saying, Thus saith Jehovah, I remember for thee the kindness of thy youth, the love of thine espousals; how thou wentest after me in the wilderness, in a land that was not sown.

Jeremiah 2:2

DIVINE MONEY SPELLS

Dragonstar ~ William Oribello

SPELL TO NEVER HAVE MONEY WORRIES AGAIN

Give no occasions of stumbling, either to Jews, or to Greeks, or to the church of God: even as I also please all men in all things, not seeking mine own profit, but the 'profit' of the many, that they may be saved.

1st Corinthians 10:32-33

SPELL FOR GOOD LUCK AND HAPPINESS

I will give thanks unto thee; for I am fearfully and wonderfully made: Wonderful are thy works; And that my soul knoweth right well.

Psalms 139:14

SPELL TO RECEIVE INTUITIVE GUIDANCE WHEN MAKING AN IMPORTANT DECISION

For I know the plans I have for you, says the Lord. They are plans for good and not for evil, to give you a future and a hope.

Jeremiah 29:11

DIVINE MONEY SPELLS
Dragonstar ~ William Oribello

KEEP POVERTY AT BAY

To keep poverty from taking everything away from you or a friend, take a length of black thread from an unused spool. Starting from the bottom, tie seven knots throughout the length of the thread and recite out loud with each knot:

For we are God's workmanship, created in Christ Jesus to do good works, which God prepared in advance for us to do.

Ephesians 2:10

Place the thread in a small bag and whoever needs it, carry it with him at all times to keep poverty away.

TO HAVE GOOD FORTUNE

This is for anyone who has been unlucky despite their best efforts. Say this Bible verse three times before the sun rises:

And they that are wise shall shine as the brightness of the firmament; and they that turn many to righteousness as the stars for ever and ever.

Daniel 12:3

DIVINE MONEY SPELLS
Dragonstar ~ William Oribello

TO LIVE HAPPY AND BE PROSPEROUS

Say this verse once a day, every day:

Thou wilt shew me the path of life; in thy presence is fullness of joy; at thy right hand there are pleasures for evermore.

Psalms 16:11

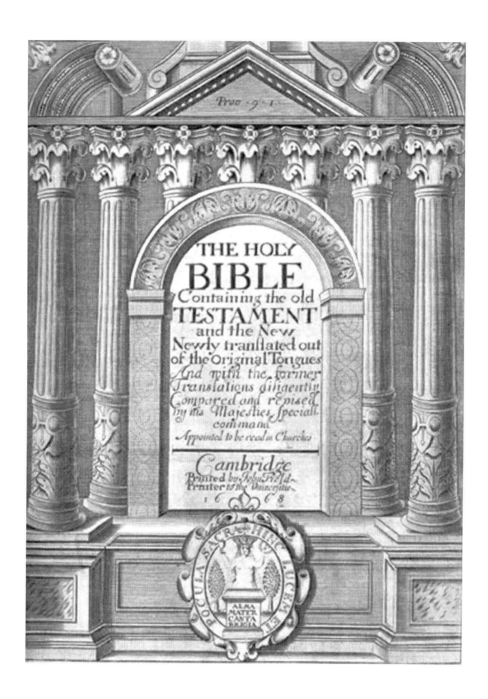

DIVINE MONEY SPELLS
Dragonstar ~ William Oribello

CHAPTER SIX - SECRETS OF GOOD FORTUNE

In this chapter I will reveal many truths about money and good fortune. You can use these truths in your daily life for more prosperity and happiness. Do the practices carefully and faithfully and you will see the results. These practices can open up new opportunities to lead you into prosperous situations.

MONEY IS GOOD

The first thing you must do is erase any idea that money is evil. Many people like to quote from the Holy Bible, the scripture which says, "The love of money is the root of all evil." After hearing this scripture many times it becomes repetitive and therefore, creates a subconscious mental block against money.

I will now explain to you what this scripture really means. The evilness of money would be to place more importance on money than on anything or anyone. Also, to love money to the point of craving or lusting after it, because one lacks it. This scripture does not mean that it is evil to have or want money.

LACK IS EVIL

To crave money because of the lack of it is the root of all evil. Many people are serving time in prison because of the lack of money. The person did not realize that their own self created limitation made it so. Therefore, they came to the conclusion that the only way to obtain money was to be dishonest. Many homes have been broken because a person became so obsessed with making money that they totally lost contact with their loved ones.

Money is not evil of itself. Money is good and can assist you in the comfort and pleasures of life. Think how wonderful

118

it would be to have enough money for everything you need and also be able to help others. Worry about money causes bad nerves and even physical illness. Money can bring peace of mind which then allows you to concentrate on important spiritual matters.

POWERFUL MONEY RITUALS

I will now share some of the universal prosperity laws with you. First I will give you the following exercises to remove any negative mental blocks you may have about money. Do them daily if it is possible.

Exercise #1: Relax your physical body. When you are relaxed, visualize yourself in a room of pure white. See a small green chest (like a jewelry box) on the floor. You may see this small chest as made of jade. On the top of this chest see the words "Money is good," in solid gold letters. Now open this chest and see money springing up out of it. It is like a fountain of water but it is money. Money of all denominations. It begins to cover the floor and pile up. Use your power of visualization to bring this money to you. After this exercise get up and forget about it until the next session.

Exercise #2: King David said in Psalms 23:1, "The Lord is my shepherd, I shall not want." A wonderful thing happens when we look to God for guidance. We, then, come to a state of living where we want for nothing but that which is good for us and those around us.

With this in mind take a small piece of paper and write the following words: *The Lord is my shepherd, I (insert your name here) shall not want.*

Place the paper where you will see it the first thing each morning and the last thing each night. Be faithful in these practices and you will soon erase all mental blocks about money.

DIVINE MONEY SPELLS
Dragonstar ~ William Oribello

SEVEN MONEY SECRETS

God's greatest secret of good fortune is contained in the combined realization and principles set forth in the seven money secrets listed below.

MONEY SECRET #1 - *Give freely to those in need. Do not wait until you are rich, give from what you have on hand.*

MONEY SECRET #2 - *Do not see what you give as coming from you. See it as coming from beyond you and fl owing through you. There is an important reason for this. If you see what you give as coming from you there will arise a fear that you may deplete yourself. This is because most people think of self as being limited. When you see what you give as only flowing through you and coming from a higher, unlimited power, the fear has to leave.*

MONEY SECRET #3 - *When you give, give from the heart. Give like you are giving to those you love the most. Do not expect anything in return. Every good deed is an Investment in the universal bank which comes back to you in time, many fold.*

MONEY SECRET #4 - *Quit thinking negative thoughts. Work on recreating your self image. See yourself as prospering in every way.*

MONEY SECRET #5 - *Quit speaking negative words. Let only positive words come from your lips, if you slip, correct yourself until positive speaking becomes a habit.*

MONEY SECRET #6 - *Spend money for what you like to do, with what you have to work with. This makes room for self satisfaction and for more riches to come into your life.*

MONEY SECRET #7 - *Observe the Golden Rule that says, "Do unto others what you would have them do unto you".*

•   •   •

These principles are the universal laws which will help change your life and draw good fortune like a magnet. Remember this scripture:

"Beloved, I wish above all things that you prosper."

The Third Epistle of John, Verse 2, (The Holy Bible).

CHAPTER SEVEN – MAKE YOUR WISHES COME TRUE

What we think, our beliefs, how we see ourselves and our world, form the framework of our reality. Our world behaves just as we expect it to – as we think it will. And we get from it what we think we deserve.

Those of us, who believe we have bad luck, are victims of the circumstances of our lives, are pawns of an uncaring, unfeeling god, and will find that bad luck will continuously follow them throughout their lives.

Every time progress is made, they will find something waiting around the corner to steal what they worked so hard to get. This happens because that is what they expect to happen. That is what they believe will be waiting for them.

On the other hand, when you realize that you are responsible for the life you have created, that you created it through your thoughts, feelings and actions — through what you believe about yourself and the world — through the fear and love you generate within and around you, you begin to discover just how much power you have to get what you want out of life.

Changing beliefs, letting go of negative thoughts and adopting a more positive "yes, I can" attitude based on beliefs that are nurturing and loving can literally make the difference between happiness and sadness, success and failure.

Today there are thousands of books on the nature of reality, consciousness, positive thinking, all written with one primary objective: to expose the conflicts in our old belief systems and provide us with new frameworks, new attitudes that affirm rather than deny our power and release us to the life of love, good health, abundance and ease that is our natural birthright.

DIVINE MONEY SPELLS
Dragonstar ~ William Oribello

Yet, at the end of the day, changing your beliefs is as easy as changing your shirt. Once you decide you can, you will. As long as you believe you cannot, you are stuck. This shows the power in our beliefs about ourselves.

Words have vibrational frequency; just as colors and numbers can be associated with a vibrational frequency, so can sounds and words. Every letter of the alphabet can be associated with a number and every number, and every color, can be associated with a musical note. When letters are strung together to form a specific sound or word, the word is "charged" in a sense, with a specific frequency that is more than the sum of its parts, and that word then, influences all who think, read, speak or hear it.

Words are even further charged as humans attach certain emotions to specific words. The bible says "In the beginning was the word," inferring that the universe, all of God's creation was created from some spoken expression, a Godly sound.

So what kind of Godly sounds are you creating day by day? And are these sounds affirming your personal happiness, or are they serving to block you from ever getting close to anything you dream of having or being in life?

When you first recognized the power of language, you can immediately see an opportunity to change your life. It does not take much for you to notice how negative your language is, and how deeply ingrained in your language is your fears and anxieties about life. Consider the negative inner chatter that fills your head every single day: "you're too fat, too slow, too stupid, too late."

All of us are guilty of a long list of inner criticisms. Unfortunately, all that inner chatter is debilitating in a very real sense. Our negative language takes us down, lowers our frequency, and makes the possible impossible.

It speaks to all your fears and blocks, all the reasons why you hold yourself back, and all the ways that you sabotaged your success. The more you listen to the words you use about yourself and your world, the more you see why you draw so much pain into your life. By this simple clarification on your negative thoughts, you can realize just how powerful simple word and thoughts actually are.

One of the first lessons you need to learn is to change your language, to start introducing "loving language" to your vocabulary. This means that you need to learn to actively listen to yourself and to others. You need to acknowledge the fears, the doubts, the pain, that your negative language represents, and then to actively shift the energy by reframing the words into affirming, loving language.

It is not enough to just work on changing the words; you can affirm yourself into big trouble if you don't pay attention. There is a reason why you are in a negative mode. You are unhappy, afraid, angry, something... something that needs to be attended to before positive affirming language can really help. However, once you acknowledge whatever that something is, once you learn to listen to yourself and notice what it is that you are afraid or resentful of, or angry or anxious about, and then also reframed the words to be more affirming, you will see that you have a very powerful tool for changing your life.

Here are some examples of our negative, unloving, low vibration language, and some ways of reframing these statements or changing the words to bring the vibration up so it attracts more of what you want in life.

LEARNING TO USE THE RIGHT WORDS

There are times when NO is the right answer, and NOT helps define a clear boundary, so there is no reason to try to eradicate these words from your vocabulary. However, there is a real need for us each to notice how often and when we are using these words, and to understand their effect on the subconscious.

DIVINE MONEY SPELLS
Dragonstar ~ William Oribello

The subconscious doesn't register qualifying, descriptive language. So when you say: "I'm not going," the subconscious registers: "I'm going."

Do you ever wonder why you ended up going to that function that you definitely had no intention of going to? The more often you said no, the more you affirmed the likelihood that you would go. That is how our kids wear us down. So, instead of saying "I'm not going," say: "I have something else to do that evening." It is a safer way of saying "no."

The same logic applies to the use of "un" and "dis" words. The subconscious hears the active part of the word and therefore nullifies to a large extent the statement you make.

When you say you are "unhappy," or you "dislike," the inner you registers that you are "happy" and you "like." Instead, try replacing the statement with something specific like, "I feel depressed about..." or "my job is unsatisfying..."

NUMBERS IN LIMBO

In 1992, a paranormal investigator named Helmut Schmidt set up a radioactive decay counter to generate sequences of random numbers, both positive and negative. The numbers were recorded, but not seen by any person. Several months later, these numbers were shown to a group of students who had been asked to use their "mind power" to skew the sequences in favor of positive numbers. Elaborate precautions were taken to prevent cheating.

According to fundamental physical laws, there should have been an equal number of positive and negative numbers. But Schmidt reported that the students saw more positive numbers; the probability of that happening was less than 1 in a 1,000. Did the students actually influence the outcome of radioactive decay rates recorded months before? Henry Stapp, a theoretical physicist at UC Berkeley, thought so.

Stapp was one of the independent monitors of Schmidt's experiments. Two years later, he published a possible explanation for what had happened. In essence, he suggested that human consciousness had interacted with the numbers, effectively altering the past (when the numbers were recorded).

The idea, which Stapp and others have since expanded upon and promoted, is that human consciousness is an unexplained, nonlinear force of nature. Like subatomic particles in quantum mechanics, the numbers in Schmidt's experiment existed in a sort of limbo in which they were positive, negative and neither until the students saw them. At that point, human consciousness and intent (instructions to think positive) induced the numbers to assume a specific condition or quantum state. Science is now coming around to the idea that thought is reality, thought has power.

The physics of consciousness is controversial, to say the least. And Stapp is first to say much more study and experimentation is necessary, especially by respected scientists in well-regarded scientific journals.

"You'd think people would want to either refute or confirm some of these reports," said Stapp, "but the only people willing to test them are people who already tend to believe them. Most mainstream labs shy away for fear of sullying their reputations, as if they would be dirtying their hands by even imagining some of this is possible."

What do you want from life? If you can think up ten things that you want right away, then most likely you would not be reading this book. However, if you are like most people, you find yourself feeling uncertain, a bit uncomfortable, or even guilty when you ask yourself that question. Why do you think that this is? After all, God wants us to be happy.

We all have been conditioned to overlook our personal wants and needs in favor of the group desires. We sublimate our thoughts, and language, hiding our true selves behind the greater good.

As time passes, most of us lose sight of what we really want, think or feel. We might be able to name the next car, house, book, dress, or computer upgrade that we want, but we won't be able to speak in specific terms about what we want for ourselves in life. Most of us simply can not find the words to express our deepest needs and desires.

Many relationships break down because partners cannot specify their needs, or are afraid to be blunt about what works and does not work for them. We hold all of these unspoken expectations of each other and of life in general, and then we wonder why we can't get what we want out of life. How do you expect anyone to satisfy your needs if you cannot speak of them? Even God wants to know what you need and want. This concept of specificity applies to all we say, think and feel. It is only with clear, specific language that we can create change.

For example, when you say "I don't like you," you leave me no room to negotiate or change your opinion. However, if you say "I don't like your taste in clothes," then I have something to work with. I can decide that pleasing you is worth taking a look at the types of clothes I wear, or I can decide that it's not important to please you on this specific issue. What is important is that by being specific about what you don't like, you affirm the possibility of change, without destroying my self-esteem.

A lack of specificity in one's language attracts a lot of static to your communications. General, uncommitted language hides the conflicts, the unresolved issues. These conflicts act like static on the line, making it difficult for folks to hear you clearly.

If words have vibrational frequency and the higher frequencies attract good stuff to you, then it makes sense to opt for using clear specific language, how else can you clearly and specifically direct the flow of energy around you to create exactly what you want?

Magick spells, curses, blessings and invocations are ways of invoking the power of words. All who teach the ceremonial use of language will also teach the need to be exceptionally clear and specific in any incantation or prayer. Otherwise, things can go terribly wrong.

We invoke the real power of language when we are clear and concise in our choice of words. The more specific you are with the words you use, the more clearly focused is the energy. And clear focused energy is at the root of every success.

So, the next time someone asks you what you want, take some time, to think about your answer and then respond with a clear specific statement: "I want a new, better paying job in six months." Or, "I want to be completely free of dept."

We also need to address the overuse of the word "should." Every time we use the word should, we are reacting to a judgment, of ourselves or others. Usually, these are unhealthy judgments, expectations that are conditioned as opposed to real.

for example: "I should work harder" – speaks to your judgment that you are lazy, are not good enough, and every time you make this statement you are driving yourself down as opposed to up. However, if, every time you hear yourself about to make this statement, you instead say: "I work smart, all my activities are productive," you will find to your amazement that you are indeed working smart and being far more productive than you have ever been

"Should" implies lack, inadequacy and fear. Shoulds reinforce a kind of poverty-consciousness of the soul. They hold us in our "nots" and discourage us from taking positive affirmative action.

DIVINE MONEY SPELLS
Dragonstar ~ William Oribello

THE ENERGY OF WORDS

The message in all of this is to seek loving language. Love energy is affirming, balancing and honest. When we learn to speak with the integrity of true love, to be specific in our choice of words, and then to choose words that are loving, positive, affirming – even in describing a challenge that we are facing – we discover an amazing power. Suddenly, with age-old problems, solutions appear, the journey to achieving goals, and finding happiness becomes a simpler, smoother path. Invoke the power of loving language in your life and then stand back to enjoy the magic that ensues.

Words have power, and loving words have the power to make life magical. So start today by looking at your words and thoughts, consider how each and every statement that you think and say can be shifted towards the positive and away from the negative. It may turn out to be the most significant change you will ever make in your life.

ENERGY WORDS EXERCIZE

Here is a simple exercise to help you start noticing your low frequency language and then to shift it to a more positive affirming vibrational frequency. You will need a notebook or journal for this exercise. For the next week, take 15 minutes every day to journal the events of the day and then five minutes to list what you want and what you are afraid of. Beginning on the second day, after you have completed your journal entries for the day, review everything you have written from the beginning of the week. Notice the negative, low-frequency language and take an additional 15 minutes to rewrite any negative statements with energy words, loving language.

By the end of the week, you will probably notice that there are far fewer low frequency words in your journal, and that you are also correcting your spoken language. As well, you will probably also notice that the week has been easier, that things came more easily to you.

It is amazing how just by changing a few words that we speak or think that our lives can be changed as well. Take the time to examine how you speak and think. Take the time to examine how the energy of your thoughts and words has a very real and significant influence on the direction that your life takes. In order to find happiness, we must first make it real in our minds and then in our words.

Our words create a perceptual filter through which we experience our world. Our words attract and create the nature of our experiences. Remember, when you say a word, any word, it produces a corresponding physical vibration that not only broadcasts out into the world, but also is recorded in your own personal frequency. Be conscious of the power of the words you use, because it is important to the rest of your life.

Imagine that your whole body is a magnificent orb of positive energy, a thought-field made up of uplifting; loving empowering words...do it now. Feel good now, because now is the beginning of the rest of your life.

DIVINE MONEY SPELLS
Dragonstar ~ William Oribello

CHAPTER EIGHT – SACRED INCENSE

Since ancient times, incense has been burned as a deity offering, spiritual cleansing, mood setting, or for magickal purposes. The Bible says in Exodus 30:1, "Thou shalt make an Altar to burn Incense on." History tells us that incense has been used as a sacrifice to the Deity, as a demonifuge to drive away evil spirits, and because people believe that it will bring good luck and enable them to gain their desires in love, money matters and other forms of magickal workings.

Our mental state and emotions can be profoundly affected by scents and fragrances. They can stimulate, calm, and regularize. To calm reduce anxiety, stress, and fear, we use incense that has a direct and relaxing influence on the psyche.

Burn incense in the evening, while listening to soft background music and candlelight, relaxing as all your tensions and troubles dissipate along with the fragrant smoke. Incense can also have stimulating as well as revitalizing effects, and may be helpful in strengthening our potential and energy when we feel weak, discouraged, or exhausted.

The practice of burning incense to accompany invocations, prayers and spells is particularly favored by practitioners of Divine Money Spells. In addition, if a spell involves a person far away, incense may be burned to "carry" the wish or desire to him or her. Incense if particularly good to help carry a spell across running water, which has a tendency to "carry" the energies of a spell away from who it was intended.

When incense is burned prior to magickal workings, fragrant smoke also purifies the surrounding area of negative and disturbing vibrations. Though such purification is not usually necessary, it does help create the appropriate mental state necessary for the successful practice of magick. When the incense is smoldered in a ritual setting it undergoes a transformation. The vibrations, no longer trapped in their physical form, are released into the environment. Their energies, mixing with those who use them, speed out to effect the changes necessary to the manifestation of the magickal goal.

The oldest and most original incenses used by mankind have been tree resins and herbs or woods that burn with a fragrant smoke. Typical herbal incenses include sage and tobacco, much favored by Native Americans and those who follow their traditions.

Sage is typically utilized in the form of wrapped and tied smudge sticks, while tobacco is burned in a ceremonial pipe. The best-known wood chip incense is the rare and expensive sandalwood, which is made of finely shaved chips of the tree of the same name. Resin incenses, which are granular lumps of dried tree sap, include the Biblical frankincense and myrrh as well as Benzoin and Copal, the latter a very special holy incense of the Mayan Indians of Central America.

Resins are often burned in mixtures, the light scent of golden frankincense combining beautifully with richly musky myrrh and sharply aromatic Benzoin. Another favorite mixture is cleansing camphor and purifying pine resin.

There are two types of incense that are used in magick: the combustible and the noncombustible. The former contains potassium nitrate (saltpeter) to aid in burning, while the latter does not. Therefore, combustible incense can be burned in the form of bricks, cones, sticks and other shapes, whereas noncombustible incense must be sprinkled onto glowing charcoal blocks to release its fragrance.

PREPARING FOR INCENSE MAGICK

Of all of the methods featured in this book, incense magick, when used with Bible verses, is probably the easiest to practice. The fragrant smoke from your incense actually does a lot of your work for you in settling your mind to focus on what you want to accomplish.

DIVINE MONEY SPELLS

Dragonstar ~ William Oribello

As well, the type of incense that you use can be entirely your personal preference. Certain types of incense can be used for various magickal desires, but for example, if you associate strawberry incense with love and romance, then by all means use strawberry incense when doing a love spell. If you cannot make up your mind, sandalwood incense is an excellent all-purpose incense that will be effective with any kind of magick spell.

As always, before you start your magick, place yourself in a quiet location so you won't be disturbed for about a half an hour. Relax and light your incense, envision the smoke rising as a caressing hand. Allow the incense to encircle your body and infuse your spirit with its wisdom and knowledge. Meditate on what you want your spell to accomplish and visualize how you will feel when your spell does its work. When you feel energized and ready, read your verse out loud three times. You can perform this spell for three days, wait three weeks, and try again if the spell does not take.

• • •

INCENSE SPELL FOR SUCCESS IN MAKING MONEY

Suggested incense: cinnamon

Bring ye all the tithes into the storehouse, that there may be meat in mine house, and prove me now herewith, saith the Lord of hosts, if I will not open you the windows of heaven, and pour you out a blessing, that there shall not be room enough to receive it.

Malachi 3:10

133

DIVINE MONEY SPELLS
Dragonstar ~ William Oribello

INCENSE SPELL TO ATTRACT WEALTH

Suggested incense: ginger

Ask me, and I will give you the nations as your inheritance and the ends of the earth as your own possession.

Psalms 2:8

INCENSE SPELL FOR LUCK WITH THE LOTTERY

Suggested incense: chamomile

Honor the Lord with your possessions and with the first fruits of all your increase; so your barns will be filled with plenty, and your vats will overflow with new wine.

Proverbs 3:9-10

INCENSE SPELL SO THAT DEBTS WILL BE REPAYED

Suggested incense: almond

Do not rob the poor because he is poor, nor oppress the afflicted at the gate; for the Lord will plead their cause, and plunder the soul of those who plunder them.

Proverbs 22:22-23

INCENSE SPELL TO GET A RAISE

Suggested incense: peony

Servants, in all things do the orders of your natural masters; not only when their eyes are on you, as pleasers of men, but

DIVINE MONEY SPELLS
Dragonstar ~ William Oribello

with all your heart, fearing the Lord: Whatever you do, do it readily, as to the Lord and not to men.

Colossians 3:22-23

INCENSE SPELL TO FIND LOST MONEY

Suggested incense: marigold

Go, and cry in the ears of Jerusalem, saying, Thus saith Jehovah, I remember for thee the kindness of thy youth, the love of thine espousals; how thou wentest after me in the wilderness, in a land that was not sown.

Jeremiah 2:2

INCENSE SPELL TO NEVER HAVE MONEY WORRIES AGAIN

Suggested incense: patchouli

Give no occasions of stumbling, either to Jews, or to Greeks, or to the church of God: even as I also please all men in all things, not seeking mine own profit, but the `profit' of the many, that they may be saved.

1st Corinthians 10:32-33

DIVINE MONEY SPELLS
Dragonstar ~ William Oribello

CHAPTER NINE – THE LOVE OF MONEY

It is often suggested that money spells teach people to love and worship money rather than making do with what they have. Is it wrong to want money in order to live ones life free of hardship and worry? Is it wrong to have enough money to feed your family and keep them safe and warm? Are we meant to live in poverty, begging on the streets, being victimized by criminals and other unsavory people?

One should not have to spend too much time considering these questions. Money is a necessary part of our society. It has been this way for hundreds of years. Some may argue that money is what leads to much of societies social problems...and we are not going to get into that debate. Right now, money is an important factor in all of our lives and there is not much we can currently do to change that. The real question is whether or not we should be using Magick in order to attract more money, prosperity and good luck into our lives.

As has been stated many times in this book, the Creator wants us to be happy, to grow and learn as not only spiritual beings, but also as physical beings. Denying ourselves the parts of our material world that keeps us alive, safe and happy is foolish and not very conducive for allowing ourselves to learn and grow.

This is of course unless you feel that eternal suffering is our fate for choosing to live in the physical world. If that is the way you feel, then peace be with you. As for all the rest, stop feeling guilty about needing money.

The real problem about money is greed. Some people can never have enough money or possessions. For these people Divine Money Spells will never work properly. The universe has ways of keeping the proper balance. It may seem that some greedy people are able to slide through life, prospering off the backs of others with no bad consequences for their hurtful actions. Rest assured that these people will have to pay their Karmic dept eventually. Do not worry about these people.

If someone has profited off of you through deceit or other harmful actions, let it go and continue on with your life. If you were meant to have the money you lost through deceit, it will return to you one way or another. If it doesn't, use it as a lesson on life, learn from the situation and grow a little as both a spiritual and a physical being.

Uses Divine Money Spells with a heart free of greed and harmful wishes towards others; the amount of money that you are meant to have will find its way to you. Be satisfied with what you receive and do not forget to help others in need as well. For sharing your wealth, no matter how much you have, with those who are less fortunate will not only make our Creator happy, it is good for your soul and the souls of our brothers and sisters.

The final pages of this book are made up of Divine Money Spells that have been sent in by followers of Dragonstar and William Oribello. These people had success with these spells and wanted to share them.

If you also have had success with certain spells, please share them to anyone who you think would need a little good fortune in their lives. You can also send them to us care of:

Global Communications
P.O. Box 753
New Brunswick, NJ   08903

DIVINE MONEY SPELLS
Dragonstar ~ William Oribello

SPELL TO GET WHAT YOU WANT

All you need are the three basic magic necessities, need, emotion, and knowledge. Concentrate on only what you need. Say the following:

I give, because I'm generous. I take because I ask.
What I well deserve is what I will get.
I deserve (whatever you need) I need (whatever you need)
I will get (whatever you need) so be it, and so it is.

TO ELIMINATE POVERTY

This is based on a New Orleans voodoo formula and you will need sugar, salt, rice, and an open safety pin. This spell will insure that you always have the staples in life. Fill a bowl with equal parts of sugar, salt, and rice. Place an open safety pin in its center. Keep the bowl out in the open to forever eliminate poverty.

DIVINE MONEY SPELLS
Dragonstar ~ William Oribello

MIRROR MAGICK

Take a small mirror and lay it down, so it reflects up at you. Then take a bowl of water (preferably a glass or silver bowl, but any bowl will do. Only use plastic bowls if you absolutely have to.

Put the bowl of water in the center of the mirror, and surround the mirror with candles (this spell should be done in a dark room or at night). The spell works best if the candles are vanilla or lavender.

There should be four candles, one at each corner of the mirror (or, if using a round mirror, one at each of these points: Northeast, Northwest, Southeast, Southwest).

In between the candles, on the North, East, South, and West sides of the mirror, put incense burners (the spell can work without the incense, but it works better with it).

Put a small piece of silver (it can be a coin, a piece of a fork, anything) in the bowl. Look down at the mirror, and chant this:

Mirror, Mirror, on the floor,
reflect for me forever more,
give me now the thing I crave,
I'll give it back when I'm in my grave,
A pool of water, A touch of ice,
a teardrop from the moon, all this I have and all I
want, Is this.

Then say out loud what it is that you need.

139

DIVINE MONEY SPELLS
Dragonstar ~ William Oribello

A MONEY SPELL

When the Moon is new, snip a piece of ivy and place it in some water for a month to grow roots. You will need some soil, a green candle, a silver coin, some thread and some money drawing oil and incense.

Anoint the candle with the oil as well as some money you won't spend and the pot for the plant. Light some charcoal. Say:

Three by three, money come to me!

Put some incense on the charcoal. Pass the candle, plant, and pot through the smoke. Put the silver coin the soil but away from the root system of where the ivy will go. Now, light the candle saying:

Money, draw to the light like a moth to the flame.
Burn away doubt and struggle and pain.
So mote it be.

Now pass the pot and plant over the flame and through the smoke again. Now, plant the ivy, saying:

As this plant grows, so will my fortune.
As this ivy grows, so will my money.
Silver multiply and bring to me,
so many riches I can finally be free.

Now, put the pot in a sunny spot where the ivy gets late day light and don't drench it but keep it wet.

DIVINE MONEY SPELLS

Dragonstar ~ William Oribello

MONEY JAR

For this spell you will need a paper and pen, seven dimes, a quart jar with screw-on lid, and one bay leaf.

Write your need on the paper and drop it into the jar. Take the seven dimes in your dominate hand and place them one by one into the jar. As each one drops, visualize it multiplying into huge amounts and say:

Toward this wish, the money grows
by leaps and bounds - it overflows.
Coins that jingle, coins that shine
come to me now - you are mine.

Write your name on the bay leaf and drop it into the jar. Screw on the lid and place the jar where you can see it everyday, but where it is not visible to everyone who enters your home.

Add a coin or two to the jar each day, and watch as money flows to you from unexpected sources. After you obtain the money you need, remove the paper and bury it outside.

MONEY, MONEY SPELL

This may be done at any time, but preferably at the same time each day or night.

You will need one green candle and one white Candle. The Green candle represents the money, and the white candle represents you. Make sure you anoint the candles with oil first, thinking of your desire for money to come to you.

DIVINE MONEY SPELLS
Dragonstar ~ William Oribello

Set the candles on your alter or table nine inches apart. After doing this say:

Money, money come to me
In abundance three times three
May I be enriched in the best of ways
Harming none on its way
This I accept, so mote it be
Bring me money three times three.

Repeat this for nine days. Each day move the white candle one inch closer to the green candle. When the candles touch, your spell is finished. Make sure you visualize the money pouring in from the universe.

SPELL FOR GOOD LUCK
Chant twice and clap hands at end:
Luck, luck, come to me, come and dance and play
with me, Fill my life with prosperity,
come, come to me!

PROSPERITY CHARM

Put a sprig of basil, a magnet and five small coins into a bag and hang above your doorway to invite prosperity.

DIVINE MONEY SPELLS
Dragonstar ~ William Oribello

WEALTH SPELL

Hold a note in your hand (ten pounds or dollars) and rub it. Burn a green/blue candle that you have purified. Imagine swimming in a pool of notes and having everything that money can buy.

Then say how much money you want and by when and then say the word: *AUM* eight times and scream: *Come to me!*

Slam your fist with the note onto the flame to put the candle out!

MONEY DOUBLING SPELL

This spells helps double any money that you have. Find some almost new paper money, a ten or twenty dollar bill is good. Place this in a white envelope, and lick, and seal it. Fold the envelope, and say once, every day, for seven days:

Universal powers to me shall bring,
The way to double this sum.
Hear me, thou spirits which sing,
Swiftly and quietly come.

Hold the envelope up and pretend that it has become heavier. Keep the envelope in your bedroom. After you receive more money, open the envelope and either spend or deposit the money.

DIVINE MONEY SPELLS
Dragonstar ~ William Oribello

MOJO BAG TO DRAW PROSPERITY

High John the Conqueror Root embodies the spirit of a heroic, fearless survivor of slavery. High John the Conqueror represents courage, strength, bravery, and the spirit of hope.

Begin this work on the waxing moon on a Thursday. Carefully select a High John the Conqueror Root that calls out to your spirit. Using your dominant hand (the most powerful hand) put root in a cup of sunflower oil. (Sunflowers possess positive energy because of their intimacy with Sun Ra). Stir in seven drops of Attar of Roses (substitute rose fragrance oil if necessary). Roses are soothing, healing plants that help us to receive blessings from the universe. Cap tightly. Swirl daily for fourteen days. Blot up any excess oil. Place fragrant High John, nutmeg, some cloves, and small cinnamon stick inside a four-by-six-inch piece of green flannel. Dip sewing needle in the sunflower and rose oil blend. Sew flannel together with green cotton thread. Feed bag at the beginning of the waxing moon and on full moon.

Food: sprinkle bag with a blend of powdered peppermint, lime, and basil (dried), magnetic sand, and sandalwood essential oil. You can also feed your money powdered High John root to draw prosperity or sprinkle it with basil.

GAMBLING MOJO HAND

This is reputed to be "The Best Gambling Hand" in the work attributed to Marie Laveau.

It is made by taking a 3.5 x 3.5 inch piece of chamois and fashioning it into a bag. Inside, you must place a small

DIVINE MONEY SPELLS
Dragonstar ~ William Oribello

lodestone, a black cat bone, a swallow's heart, a pinch of five finger grass, a small John the Conqueror root, and some devil's shoestring root.

On top of all this you must place a prepared nutmeg, which is made by hollowing out a large whole nutmeg and filling it with Lady Luck Oil, then sealing it in place with wax.

With the bag filled, sew it all shut. To activate the mojo hand, apply 3 drops of Jockey Club perfume, and dress it with another 3 drops every week thereafter.

PSALM PRAYER FOR MONEY

A simple spell to draw money and prosperity to you is to first anoint yourself with a little money drawing oil such as cedarwood or bayberry. Next, upon arising from bed, recite the 23rd psalm for seven days.

PSALM 23

The Lord is my shepherd; I shall not want.
He maketh me to lie down in green pastures.
He leadeth me beside the still waters.
He restoreth my soul.
He leadeth me in the paths of righteousness for His name's sake.
Yea, though I walk through the valley of the shadow of death,
I will fear no evil for thou art with me.
Thy rod and Thy staff they comfort me.
Thou preparest a table before me in the presence of mine enemies.
Thou anointest my head with oil.
My cup runneth over.

DIVINE MONEY SPELLS
Dragonstar ~ William Oribello

Surely goodness and mercy shall follow me all the days of my life, and I will dwell in the house of the Lord for ever.
Amen.

Money will arrive shortly thereafter to those who are truly deserving.

DIVINE WORD TO BRING MONEY

This is a very powerful money spell and does not require any rituals or ceremonies. Whenever you have any type of money problems and nothing is working for you, just pray these words:

YAA ALLAHO

You may say these magic words when ever you have time, while traveling, when ever you are alone.

If you are in the house and getting bored or when you are trying to sleep whenever possible just say these magic words, these words will work for you and will solve all your money problems forever.

As well, you can repeat this Bible verse once a day to free yourself from any problems with money.

I will also make it a possession for the bittern, and pools of water: and I will sweep it with the besom of destruction, saith the LORD of hosts.

Isaiah 14:23

DIVINE MONEY SPELLS
Dragonstar ~ William Oribello

HOW TO ATTRACT SUCCESS TO YOUR BUSINESS

All of the measures below are calculated to draw customers, and thusly success, to you and your business.

In New Orleans it is believed that Saint Peter governs business because he carries keys. Get up early in the morning and light a white candle to Saint Peter. Then mix green herbs into a bucket of water...especially parsley and thyme.

Begin mopping the floor from the front of your business toward the back, moving backwards as you go. When you reach the back of your business, burn some green incense.

Get up early and burn mixture of sulfur and sugar and money drawing incense. As the sun rises, look to the east and pray for customers to be drawn to you.

Go to the graveyard and get nine handfuls of dirt. Back home, mix it with brimstone, sulfur, red pepper, and salt. Burn the mixture and pray for success in business.

HOODOO MONEY SPELL

Materials needed: small black cotton bag, a silver dime, a nickel, and a penny, dirt from crossroads, red brick dust (made by crushing a brick), water from a river, sunlight, a piece of green string.

Begin reciting the single verse of Psalm 15:5. You will continue repeating this over and over until all of the materials are in the bag.

Place the nickel in the bag, then place the dirt in the bag, then the dime, then the brick dust, then the penny.

Tie up the top of the bag so nothing can get out with a piece of green string.

Immerse the bag in the river water and begin reciting Psalm 15:5 again. Hold it under and keep reciting Psalm 15:5 for twenty seconds before taking it back out.

Let the bag dry out in the sunlight. Make sure it is completely dry.

Sleep with the bag under your bed until the money comes.

CORN WEALTH SPELL

For wealth and prosperity for a year, take the husk from an ear of corn and put a dollar bill along with a note written on parchment:

Oh, dear god of luck,
money is like muck,
not good except it be spread.
Spread some here at_____(write in your address).
Thanks be to thee. Amen.

Sign your name. Sprinkle the dollar bill and note with Coltsfoot leaves. Roll the husk up and tie together with green string or ribbon. Hang the token up above the entryway with green cord. That husk should bring riches into your home or business by the bushel.

DIVINE MONEY SPELLS
Dragonstar ~ William Oribello

MONEY SPELL WITH SMARTWEED

To find money, one should make a conjure bag containing a magnetic horseshoe, and a lodestone to attract and draw wealth to you. You will also need some Smartweed to enable you to see how to capture it and hold it without being led astray by unprofitable distractions or foolish delays.

Feed your money bag with a sprinkle of Gold Magnetic Sand every third day until you find the amount you need.

LAVENDER MONEY SPELL

A lucky money spell is made by placing in a conjure bag seven pieces of money, each different, such as a penny, nickel, dime, quarter, a half dollar, $1.00 bill, and $5.00 bill, all of which are sprinkled liberally with lavender.

Take the bag with you for seven days and your money should multiply seven times (this would give you $41.46 above your original investment) or, in some instances, seven times seven. This would result in a tidy sum of $338.50.

LUCK HAND ROOT MONEY SPELL

To get and hold a job, always carry a Lucky Hand Root on your person. Use Lucky Nine Oil on your wrists each day for nine days, and burn some John the Conqueror Incense each night. These roots bring luck in all undertakings and no conjure bag would be considered complete without one.

The hands are usually imperfect, but this does not affect their value as a talisman. The ones which are formed so that all five fingers are distinguishable are very rare.

BLACK SNAKE ROOT SPELL TO GAIN MONEY

This spell should be done during Waxing or Full Moon.

Soak Black Snake Root, also known as Black Cohosh and Squaw Root, in a cup of boiling water for fifteen minutes. The water is then strained and the root is thrown away. The liquid is put in a bottle and left for seven days.

On the eighth day, it is rubbed over the bottom of one's shoes so that the anointed will be led toward money; to either find it, win it, or gain it in some legal manner.

USE DREAMS TO ACHIEVE WEALTH AND PROSPERITY
How to Receive Oracles by Dreams

He who would receive true dreams, should keep a pure, undisturbed, and imaginative spirit, and so compose it that it may be made worthy of knowledge and government by the mind; for such a spirit is most fit for prophesying, and is a most clear glass of all images which flow everywhere from all things. When, therefore, we are sound in body, not disturbed in mind, our intellect not made dull by heavy meats and strong drink, not sad through poverty, not provoked through lust, not incited by any vice, nor stirred up by wrath or anger, not being irreligiously and profanely inclined, not given to levity nor lost to drunkenness, but, chastely going to bed, fall asleep, then our pure and divine soul being free from all the evils above recited, and separated from all hurtful thoughts-and now freed, by dreaming is endowed with this divine spirit as an instrument, and doth receive those beams and representations which are darted down, as it were, and shine forth from, the divine Hind into itself, in a deifying glass.

There are four kinds of true dreams, viz., the first, matutine, i.e., between sleeping and waking; the second, that which one sees concerning another; the third, that whose interpretation is shown to the same dreamer in the nocturnal vision; and, lastly, that which-is related to the same dreamer in the nocturnal vision. But natural things and their own co-mixtures do likewise belong unto wise men, and we often use such to receive oracles from a spirit by a dream, which are either by perfumes, unctions, meats, drinks, rings, seals, etc.

Now those who are desirous to receive oracles through a dream, let them make themselves a ring of the Sun or Saturn for this purpose. There are likewise images of dreams, which, being put under the head when going to sleep, doth effectually give true dreams of whatever the mind hath before determined or consulted upon, the practice of which is as follows:

Thou Shalt make an image of the Sun, the figure whereof must be a man sleeping upon the bosom of an angel; which thou shall make when Leo ascends, the Sun being in the ninth house in Aries; then you must write upon the figure the name of the effect desired, and in the hand of the angel the name and character of the intelligence of the Sun, which is Michael.

Let the same Image be made in Virgo ascending-- Mercury being fortunate in Aries in the ninth, or Gemini ascending, Mercury being fortunate in the ninth house in

Aquarius and let him be received by Saturn with a fortunate aspect, and let the name of the spirit (which is Raphael) be written upon it. Let the same likewise be made-Libra ascending, Venus being received from Mercury in Gemini in the ninth house-and write upon it the name of the angel of Venus (which is Anacl). Again you may make the same image-Aquarius ascending, Saturn fortunately possessing the ninth in his exaltation, which is Libra-and let there be written upon it the name of the angel of Saturn (which is Cassial). The same may be made with Cancer ascending, the Moon being received by Jupiter and Venus in Pisces, and being fortunately placed in the ninth house-and write upon it the spirit of the Moon (which is Gabriel).

There are likewise made rings of dreams of wonderful efficacy, and there are rings of the Sun and Saturn-and the constellation of them in, when the Sun or Saturn ascend in their exaltation in the ninth, and when the Moon is joined to Saturn in the ninth, and in that sign which was the ninth house of the nativity, and write and engrave upon the rings the name of the spirit of the Sun or Saturn; and by these rules you may know how and by what means to constitute more of yourself.

But know this, that such images work nothing (as they are simply images), except they are vivified by spiritual and celestial virtue, and chiefly by the ardent desire and firm intent of the soul of the operator. But who can give a soul to an image, or make a stone, or metal, or clay, or wood, or wax, or paper, to live? Certainly no man whatever; for this arcanum doth not enter into an artist of a stiff neck. He only hath it who transcends the progress of angels, and comes to the very Archtype Himself. The tables of numbers likewise confer to the receiving of oracles, being duly formed under their own constellations.

Therefore, he who is desirous of receiving true oracles by dreams, let him abstain from supper, from drink, and be otherwise well disposed, so his brain will be free from turbulent vapors; let him also have his bed-chamber fair and clean, exorcised and consecrated; then let him perfume the same with some convenient fumigation, and let him anoint his temples with some unguent efficacious hereunto, and put a ring of dreams upon his finger; then let him take one of the images we have spoken of, and place the same under his head; then let him address himself to sleep, meditating upon that thing which he desires to know. So shall he receive a most certain and undoubted oracle by a dream when the Moon goes through the sign of the ninth revolution of his nativity, and when she is in the ninth sign from the sign of perfection.

This is the way whereby we may obtain all sciences and arts whatsoever, whether astrology, occult philosophy, physic, etc. or else suddenly and perfectly with a true Illumination of our Intellect, although all inferior familiar spirits whatsoever conduce to this effect, and sometimes also evil spirits sensibly inform us, intrinsically and extrinsically.

IN CONCLUSION THE FOLLOWING MORNING PRAYER IS GIVEN, WHICH IS TO BE SPOKEN UPON ARISING. IT PROTECTS AGAINST ALL MANNER OF BAD LUCK.

Oh, Jesus of Nazareth, King of the Jews, yea, a King over the whole world, protect me [name] during this day and night, protect me at all times by thy five holy wounds, that I may not be seized and bound. The Holy Trinity guard me, that no gun, fire-arm, ball or lead, shall touch my body; and that they shall be weak like the tears and bloody sweat of Jesus Christ, in the name of God the Father, the Son and the Holy Ghost. Amen.

If you enjoyed this book, write for our free catalog:

Global Communications
P.O. Box 753
New Brunswick, NJ   08903

www.conspiracyjournal.com

Made in the USA
Middletown, DE
05 November 2015